IMAGES
of America

TONOPAH TEST RANGE

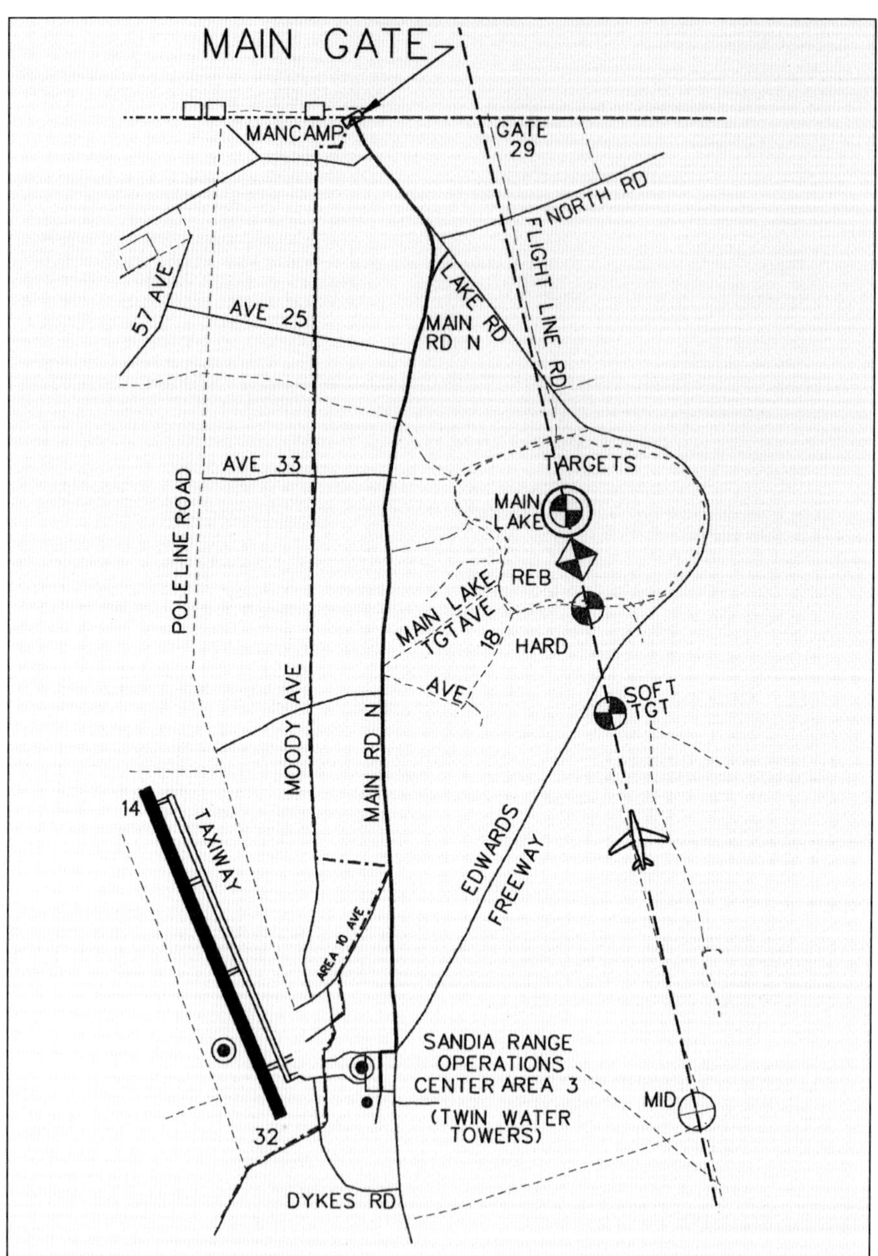

This map of the central portion of the Tonopah Test Range shows personnel accommodations (known as the man camp), target areas on a dry lakebed, the range operations center, and the airfield. Located 32 miles southeast of Tonopah, Nevada, this unique outdoor laboratory is shared by the Department of Energy and the US Air Force for weapons testing and development. (Department of Energy.)

On the Cover: The crew of a B-1B bomber performs a low-altitude laydown drop of a dummy B83 nuclear weapon shape. The parachute is designed to slow the 2,400-pound bomb long enough to allow the delivery aircraft to escape prior to detonation. The B83 was among the last megaton-yield weapons in the nation's nuclear stockpile. (US Air Force.)

IMAGES
of America

TONOPAH TEST RANGE

Peter W. Merlin

ISBN 978-1-4671-0579-8

Published by Arcadia Publishing
Charleston, South Carolina

Printed in the United States of America

Library of Congress Control Number: 2020945055

For all general information, please contact Arcadia Publishing:
Telephone 843-853-2070
Fax 843-853-0044
E-mail sales@arcadiapublishing.com
For customer service and orders:
Toll-Free 1-888-313-2665

Visit us on the Internet at www.arcadiapublishing.com

From left to right, Eric LeVeque, Tom Kinzel, and the author (standing by his 1991 Jeep Cherokee) visited the Tonopah Test Range sign in May 1993 during a road trip through Nevada. The "rocket" topping the sign was apparently cobbled together from the bottom half of a Nike Ajax missile and a dummy B57 nuclear bomb shape. (Author's collection.)

Contents

Acknowledgments

After writing Arcadia histories of the Nevada Test Site and Area 51, I thought it would be appropriate to document the story of the lesser known but equally fascinating Tonopah Test Range.

As always, I owe a debt of gratitude to a number of individuals as well as to numerous federal and corporate historians and archivists. I offer special thanks to the outstanding people at Arcadia Publishing, including Stacia Bannerman and others, without whom this project would not have been possible, and to my wife, Sarah, for copyediting my draft manuscript.

Unless otherwise noted, images in this book are courtesy of Sandia National Laboratories. Other sources include the US Air Force (USAF), National Nuclear Security Administration/Nevada Field Office (NNSA/NV), Department of Energy (DOE), National Aeronautics and Space Administration (NASA), Lockheed Martin Skunk Works (LMSW), Red Eagles Alumni Association (REAA), and various individual contributors.

INTRODUCTION

In the mid-1950s, the Atomic Energy Commission (AEC) surveyed numerous sites in the western United States for possible use as a permanent ballistic test range for unarmed nuclear weapon shapes. Most were rejected for reasons ranging from unsatisfactory terrain to population density and land ownership conflicts. In February 1956, a study conducted by the Naval Air Special Weapons Facility recommended a location in the northwest corner of the Las Vegas Bombing and Gunnery Range that included a string of dry lakebeds about 32 miles southeast of the town of Tonopah, Nevada. Known as Cactus Flat, this site was remote and isolated and had reasonably good weather throughout the year.

Initially, the AEC secured only right-of-entry and temporary use of a 369,280-acre parcel of land. The Air Force then issued a permit to Sandia Laboratory (designated Sandia National Laboratories by Congress in 1979) for use of the range from November 1956 to November 1961. Construction of facilities and infrastructure began in the fall of 1956.

The test complex was inaugurated in February 1957 with drop tests of two nuclear weapon shapes from bombers operating out of Kirtland Air Force Base, New Mexico. These missions demonstrated that Tonopah Test Range (TTR), which later appeared on AEC maps as Area 52, was more than adequate for high- and low-altitude bombing operations.

In late 1958, the AEC decided to make TTR a permanent facility. Plans for expansion and improvement were drawn up and received approval a few months later. In April 1959, the Air Force extended the permit covering Sandia's use of the area for the next decade.

During the 1960s, the TTR mission evolved to include rocket launch capabilities for testing parachute systems and shock-resistant components. Later requirements resulted in the emplacement of 155-millimeter and 203-millimeter guns to test artillery-fired atomic projectile (AFAP) designs. TTR also became a primary site for high-explosive studies during the early phases of Project Plowshare, an attempt to develop peaceful uses for nuclear explosives. Other experiments included underground blast effects, explosive case ruptures, shockwave studies, cratering tests, and overpressure measurements. In January 1963, the Air Force Flight Test Center (AFFTC) and AEC signed a memorandum of understanding that allowed AFFTC to use part of the TTR airspace for X-15 rocket plane operations in the vicinity of Mud Lake.

In the spring of 1963, several weapon safety experiments, commonly known as plutonium dispersal tests, took place at TTR as part of a joint US-British program called Operation Roller Coaster. In these tests, nuclear warheads were subjected to simulated accidents in which only one or a few detonators fired. Although these asymmetrical detonations precluded nuclear explosions, the conventional high-explosive blasts spread pulverized plutonium debris over wide swaths of the test range.

The first such test, code-named Double Tracks, was executed on Stonewall Flat some 13 miles east of the town of Goldfield and 26 miles southeast of Tonopah on May 15, 1963. As predicted, there was no nuclear yield, but southerly winds deposited debris in a mile-long plume 600 feet wide, and some airborne radioactivity was detected offsite.

The next three tests were storage/transportation safety experiments conducted on Cactus Flat. The first of these, dubbed Clean Slate I, was executed on May 25. It deposited a narrow, mile-long plume of radioactive debris about 31 miles east of Goldfield. Clean Slate II, on May 31, contaminated a patch of land nearly half a square mile in area about 34 miles east of Goldfield. Clean Slate III, on June 9, produced the largest debris plume yet. It extended nearly two miles from ground zero, about 34 miles east of Goldfield. All three Clean Slate tests resulted in radioactivity being detected outside the range boundaries.

Sandia ultimately transformed TTR into a highly instrumented outdoor laboratory, with range instrumentation evolving to accommodate increasingly sophisticated test requirements. Mobile optical instruments provided greater flexibility of coverage, supplementing tracking telescopes and high-speed cameras. Three precision instrumentation radars were added to the range in 1962 and 1971 and a modified Nike-Hercules tracking system in 1976. Aided by an advanced computing complex, these systems provided accurate vehicle-acquisition vectors to instrumentation stations and controlled the optical tracking systems.

The rocket launch facility began as a single assembly building and launcher. It eventually grew to include two instrumentation bunkers, a high-explosive assembly building, and five launch sites capable of handling vehicles ranging from diminutive Loki-Dart sounding rockets up to 5,800-pound Honest John surface-to-surface missiles.

As TTR grew, a power distribution system was installed to provide commercial electrical power to all major facilities, including an instrumented gun bunker, data recording equipment, and telemetry stations. The AFAP gun mounts were built at the same time, allowing remote positioning of the fixed-azimuth guns to a 90-degree elevation. A gun support facility for temperature conditioning of projectiles and powder, shell assembly, and powder handling was completed in 1972. The following year, a rocket motor test facility was built to accommodate engines with up to 400,000 pounds of thrust. A rocket-sled track was built in 1975 to support a program for evaluating nuclear power reactor vulnerability to tornado-driven debris. This complex was later enlarged to assess vulnerability of the reactor in the event of turbine breakup.

Range facilities were upgraded in accordance with requirements for improved data collection and to provide better operating and maintenance facilities for instrumentation. Improvements included addition of a photo-optics laboratory with a clean room and film processing facilities, a new master range-timing system, and additional access roads. Additionally, a variety of hard and soft targets were marked or constructed on and near the dry lakebeds.

The remote location of TTR necessitated provisions for access by air as well as by ground transportation. A crude 5,000-foot airstrip was constructed during the 1960s for delivery of supplies and personnel. Sandia Strip, as it was known, was later extended and repaved but remained largely a bare field until the late 1970s, when the Air Force began using TTR for aircraft testing and evaluation.

In May 1978, the deputy secretary of defense approved $7 million to fund phase-one construction of a new airfield and support facilities at TTR for the 4477th Test and Evaluation Flight (TEF), the Red Eagles. Improvements included new hangars and other buildings, a concrete parking apron, a taxiway, and personnel accommodations. Sandia Strip was extended to 10,000 feet and equipped with arresting barriers and systems for navigation and instrument landings. This work was completed in June 1979.

Phase two of construction began in September 1980 at a cost of $18 million. It included expansion of the parking apron and construction of another taxiway, a dining hall, tanks for fuel and water storage, a warehouse, support utilities, and additional hangar space. Completion in January 1982 began the transition of the TTR airfield to a standard Air Force base.

The Red Eagles began as a small organization under command of the 57th Fighter Weapons Wing of Tactical Air Command (TAC). The unit's mission was tactical evaluation of foreign fighter aircraft at Area 51, some 65 miles southeast of TTR. The Red Eagles' mission expanded exponentially when Air Force headquarters directed the initiation of Project Constant Peg in January 1978. This unique program was designed to enhance warfighter readiness through tactical evaluation of foreign aircraft and to provide air-to-air combat training for airmen from the Air Force, Navy, and Marine Corps. This concept allowed US combat pilots a chance to see actual threat aircraft under realistic circumstances and gain combat experience against them. The Red Eagles, equipped with MiG-17 and MiG-21 aircraft flown by pilots trained in Soviet-style tactics, moved their operation from Area 51 to TTR on July 17, 1979.

In May 1980, the 4477th TEF was redesignated the 4477th Test and Evaluation Squadron (TES). Six months later, the squadron received the first of several MiG-23 aircraft. The MiG-17s were retired in April 1982; two had been lost in accidents, and those remaining were permanently grounded. One MiG-23 was also wrecked. Despite these incidents, the TAC inspector general rated the management, organization, and mission capability of the 4477th TES as excellent, and in June 1985, the Red Eagles received the Joint Meritorious Unit Award. For exceptionally meritorious service in previous years, the squadron also received the Air Force Outstanding Unit Award and a second Joint Meritorious Unit Award.

In March 1988, Constant Peg was discontinued due to budget cuts, and the 4477th TES was inactivated on July 15, 1990. The squadron's remaining assets and some personnel were reconstituted as Detachment 2 of the 57th Fighter Weapons Wing (FWW). This small unit underwent a great deal of reorganization over the next several years, eventually becoming Detachment 3 of the 53rd Test and Evaluation Group (TEG) in October 1996.

Detachment 3, 53rd TEG, was the designated representative for Air Combat Command (ACC) interest in Air Force foreign materiel exploitation (FME) and training opportunities with Air Force Materiel Command (AFMC). The detachment's primary mission was to ensure that Air Force combat aircrews were prepared to fight with the latest knowledge available through FME. Detachment 3, 53rd TEG, maintained active involvement with AFMC and other services ensuring that all testing was planned, executed, and reported on with combat aircrews in mind. In addition, the detachment acted as liaison for all training opportunities conducted on the Nevada Test and Training Range, providing procedures and acting as subject matter experts on key systems.

The Red Eagles had not been alone at the TTR airfield. In March 1981, phase three construction began in preparation for operational testing and evaluation of the top-secret Lockheed F-117A Nighthawk, the first operational low-observable ("stealthy") attack aircraft. Facilities were built at a cost of $79 million for the 4450th Tactical Group (TG), the unit that would operate this revolutionary aircraft. Rumors of the base's new tenant eventually leaked out, bringing some notoriety to the nearby town of Tonopah.

The 4450th TG began moving personnel to TTR in June 1981, and the first operational F-117A was accepted 15 months later. The unit achieved initial operational capability on October 28, 1983, with the delivery of the 14th operational aircraft. The group included a squadron of A-7s at Nellis Air Force Base just outside Las Vegas, which provided cover for the clandestine operation and two F-117A squadrons at TTR. Air Force personnel commuted to the base via chartered Key Air Boeing 727 aircraft on Monday mornings and returned to Nellis on Friday afternoons. Contractors arrived via Boeing 737s operated by government contractors. The Air Force commuter airlift contract was eventually taken over by American Trans Air. Sandia and Department of Energy (DOE) employees commuted to the range aboard a DC-9 operated by Ross Aviation.

The 4450th TG was inactivated in October 1989 and the component units reorganized and activated as the 37th Tactical Fighter Wing (TFW). At the same time, Detachment 1 of the 57th FWW was established at TTR for F-117A operational testing and evaluation. F-117A aircraft from TTR were deployed to Saudi Arabia in 1990 for combat missions during Operation Desert Storm. After returning from the Persian Gulf, the 37th TFW moved to Holloman Air Force Base, New Mexico.

The portion of the range operated by Sandia continued to provide research and development test support for weapons systems and components, and the Department of Defense (DoD) approved the use of TTR by military and contractor test forces on a temporary, noncontinuous basis. DOE programs included airdrops for developmental testing and stockpile sampling of a variety of nuclear weapons. Other payloads were carried aloft on Honest John, Malemute, Terrier, Zuni, and Zap rockets for weapon development tests and high-altitude experiments. The gun area fired developmental test shots for both the W79 and W82 artillery rounds. In addition, a smoothbore, recoilless Davis gun was used to fire earth penetrators into natural or man-made targets for terradynamic testing. Support for the Army included firings of non-nuclear 155-millimeter artillery rounds, tests of the Multiple Launch Rocket System, and tracking of the Electronic Warfare/Close Air Support System. In 1988, NASA used the range for air drops of an F-111 escape capsule parachute test vehicle equipped with a decelerator system developed at Sandia. For the Navy, TTR personnel performed tracking and data acquisition for flights of the Tomahawk sea-launched cruise missile. The Air Force used the range for tracking AGM-86B air-launched cruise missiles, testing the B-52H offensive avionics system, launches of the AGM-69 Short-Range Attack Missile, and a drop test of a 4,000-pound laser-guided "bunker buster" that dug a hole so deep the test article was never recovered.

In September 2005, the 57th Operations Group activated the 30th Reconnaissance Squadron at TTR to develop advanced concepts and validate tactics, techniques, and procedures for integrating remotely piloted aircraft systems into the nation's warfighting capabilities. The squadron was moved south to Creech Air Force Base, Indian Springs, Nevada, in August 2011. Responsibility for the TTR airfield was transferred from ACC to AFMC in 2012 under Detachment 3, AFFTC.

After 27 years of service, the F-117A Nighthawk returned to TTR but not as an operational combat aircraft. Air Force officials decided to accelerate retirement of the stealth fighter to free up funding for force modernization, including employment of the F22A Raptor. Surviving aircraft of the F-117A fleet were ferried to TTR between 2006 and 2008 for final storage and disposition. Several of these were retained in flyable condition and used for a variety of classified tests.

Over the years, the National Nuclear Security Administration (NNSA) and DOE conducted numerous studies to determine the feasibility of closing the range but repeatedly concluded that the flight test mission at TTR was vital to national security. Although the nuclear weapons flight test mission could be transferred to the DoD and performed elsewhere, programmatic risks and associated costs to make the transition far outweighed the benefits. In December 2008, the NNSA issued a record of decision calling for continuation of flight test activities at TTR, revitalization of some facilities and infrastructure, and changes to the overall concept of operations.

At the height of the Cold War, the range conducted approximately 300 developmental and stockpile surveillance flight tests each year, and Sandia maintained five departments with senior managers. By 2010, the lab was conducting only about a dozen stockpile-surveillance flight tests and a few work-for-others test series of four to six weeks' duration. Personnel included just 22 Sandia employees and about 90 contractors who provided site support (security, maintenance and operations, medical, fire, rescue, and hazardous materials response). Sandia therefore instituted a new business model of operating in a "campaign mode," with a small staff assigned full-time to keep the range operational supported by a cadre of Sandia employees and contractors to staff the site during test operations.

Nevertheless, as the only NNSA-dedicated flight test range, TTR remained a national asset with unique facilities and capabilities. This was reflected in Pres. Barack Obama's fiscal year 2011 congressional budget request, which specifically cited TTR's unique capabilities. Additionally, Air Force test activities were increasing in support of new aircraft and electronic warfare capabilities. Unquestionably, TTR is a critical component in the development and acquisition of future weapon systems as well as supporting legacy stockpile surveillance, assessment, and certification of nuclear armaments.

One

SANDIA TEST RANGE

A B-52 drops an unarmed B83 bomb over a target at TTR; the metal tetrahedron at lower right is a radar reflector to pinpoint the target center. The test range was established primarily for evaluating the ballistic characteristics of nuclear weapon shapes but has since evolved to provide operational and developmental testing of weapon components and assemblies in realistic environments.

The original Sandia logo was created in 1955 from a design submitted by employee Clyde Walker. It featured a mythical thunderbird from Native American folklore. The corporation was created in 1949 as a subsidiary of AT&T to manage the original laboratory in Albuquerque, New Mexico, and later the TTR field test site in Nevada.

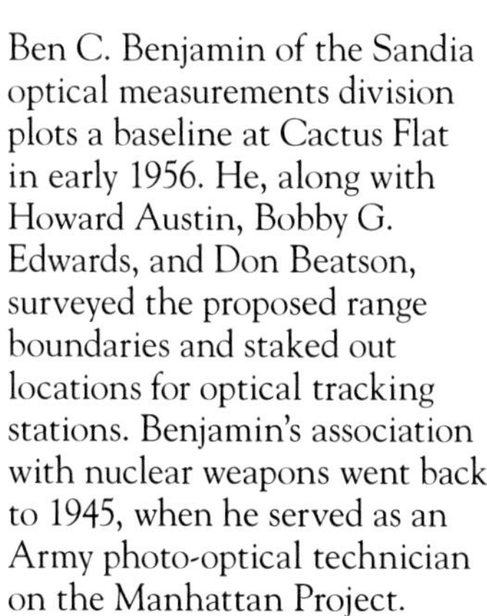

Ben C. Benjamin of the Sandia optical measurements division plots a baseline at Cactus Flat in early 1956. He, along with Howard Austin, Bobby G. Edwards, and Don Beatson, surveyed the proposed range boundaries and staked out locations for optical tracking stations. Benjamin's association with nuclear weapons went back to 1945, when he served as an Army photo-optical technician on the Manhattan Project.

Workers from Reynolds Electrical and Engineering Company (REECo) began construction at TTR Area 3 in 1956. Originally known as the Tonopah Ballistics Range, TTR was only intended to be a temporary facility to be replaced later by a ballistics range near Winslow, Arizona. The Tonopah site soon proved ideal, however, and was made permanent.

Workers are framed by the metal skin of a tower at Station 4, destined to hold an Askania phototheodolite tracking device. Tracking stations like this one sprouted like grain silos on hilltops and in valleys throughout TTR to enable collection of trajectory data from test articles dropped from airplanes or launched on rockets.

The Area 3 Control Point, as it looked in 1957, was the heart of the new test range. Construction began on August 27, 1956, and was completed three months later at a cost of $490,000. The original facilities consisted primarily of metal Butler buildings shipped from Albuquerque to Tonopah, cinetheodolite tracking equipment, an electric power generator, and a 600-foot-deep water well.

Test operations were controlled and coordinated from the Control Point in Area 3. Test conductors and other specialists manned a variety of consoles equipped with video monitors. Computer-driven plotting boards provided real-time tracking data for use by range safety personnel and allowed engineers to evaluate flight performance of aircraft and test articles.

The first permanent facilities were built by Las Vegas–based Lembke Construction in 1960. By 1961, the Control Point included five buildings: control center, administration, range maintenance facility, vehicle garage, and warehouse. There were also 17 optical tracking stations. From 1957 through 1964, TTR performed 680 bomb drops and 555 rocket launches.

An aerial view of the Control Point area in 1967 shows little noticeable change. Throughout the 1960s, TTR hosted an average of 500 tests annually, reaching a peak of 1,100 tests in a single year in the middle of the decade. The most significant challenge was recruiting personnel to work in such a remote location.

Security inspector J. Carroll checks William L. Bierly and Thomas E. Sellers through the Control Point gate during unusually inclement weather in February 1962. Testing requirements led to expansion of facilities and staffing. By the mid-1960s, there were about 40 Sandia range crew on site as well as 20 contract security guards and 50 REECo operations support and range maintenance personnel.

When Federal Services Inc. security guards Harry Schnarer, Tim Lydon, and Kessie Hall hoisted the Stars and Stripes over TTR on April 1, 1963, they included a second flag designed by Walter K. Vallely that featured a silhouette of a squirrel. Sandia personnel at TTR were nicknamed "squirrels," and Vallely made the unofficial banner to honor range boss—and "chief squirrel"—Bob Statler.

Air Force observers watch as a B-58A makes a low pass by a cinetheodolite station in 1964. The supersonic bomber was one of many aircraft tested at the range, mostly to demonstrate nuclear weapon compatibility and release characteristics. The large pod beneath the airplane's centerline was a combination weapon pod and external fuel tank for extended range. (USAF.)

This is an Askania phototheodolite without its protective dome. Ballistics engineers initially favored these precision optical instruments for recording the flight path and trajectory of bombs, missiles, and aircraft as a series of points on photographic plates. They were later replaced by cinetheodolites that recorded the test article on motion picture film.

Station 2, due west of the main target area, held a 16-inch Newtonian telescope with a focal length of 117.5 inches. There were eight of these ME-16 units at TTR, four at fixed sites like this one and four on mobile mounts. The ME-16 had a tracking rate of around 18 degrees per second.

Silhouetted by the desert sun, Lance Wilson adjusts precision optics on one of TTR's numerous tracking telescopes. The Sandia photometrics group used a variety of high-speed and special-purpose cameras for gathering data on rocket launches, weapons release characteristics, ballistics, ground impact, and explosion tests. Some of these systems were operated manually and others remotely.

Six permanently defined targets were marked or constructed along a flight line through the range following a string of dry lakebeds on Cactus Flat. Three of these were on or adjacent to Main Lake, at lower left, with others farther south at intervals all the way to Antelope Lake. (Jeff Swearingen.)

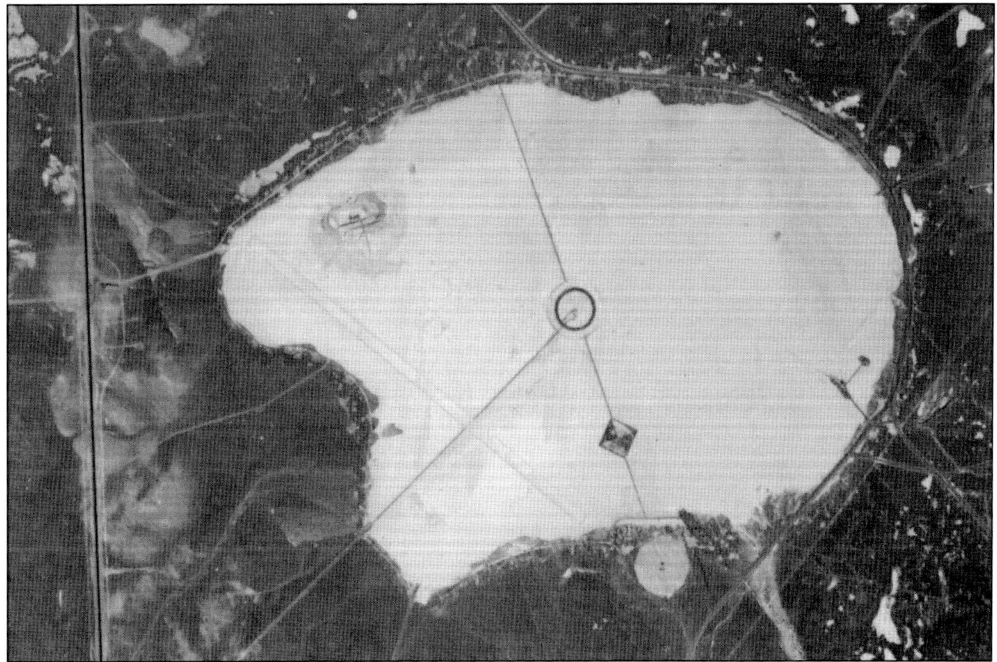

Sandia workers initially dubbed this playa Pork Lake but later changed the name to Main Lake as it became central to ballistic testing. The first targets were marked on the clay surface using road oil. Later, more permanent mixtures that could better withstand weathering were used. A concrete target was built on the south shoreline in 1961. (NNSA/NV.)

Construction of the hard target began in 1960. Nuclear weapons were originally intended for high-altitude delivery, but low-altitude penetration tactics required laydown delivery by high-speed aircraft flying at low levels to avoid detection by enemy radar. The hardened casings and impact-resistant components of laydown weapons had to be tested against a concrete surface.

As completed in 1961, the hard target was X-shaped to provide a rough approximation of two runways with an area of 250,000 square feet and a marker pole in the center of a quartered circle. A variety of laydown bombs were tested here to evaluate the survivability of impact-hardened components, parachute-delayed delivery, spike and honeycomb impact-absorbent nose cones, and other features. Main Lake Target is visible in the background.

This aerial view shows the hard target in the foreground after it was filled out into a 750-foot diameter circle of one-foot-thick concrete with a strength rating of 4,000 pounds per square inch. The quartered diamond of Rebel Target and the double ring of Main Lake Target were marked on the clay surface of the lakebed, seen here after a rainstorm. Soil composition and target construction offered a variety of surface conditions for testing, including sandy soil, hard-packed clay, and concrete. Gravel and rocky or solid rock impact areas were also available when required. Farther south along the test range flight line, Mid Target offered desert turf with a checkerboard pattern of 100-foot-wide squares. Pedro and Antelope Lake Targets had clay surfaces of varying consistency. The target areas were surrounded by cameras and other instrumentation to record weapon impacts from all angles.

The first commuter air service to the range for Sandia, AEC, and other contractor personnel was introduced in February 1961. Alamo Airlines operated a 24-seat Douglas DC-3 from Las Vegas to Tonopah Airport, a former World War II training base about 12 miles from TTR. Direct flights began in 1963. Carco Air Service picked up the contract in March 1969, replacing the DC-3 with a 44-seat Fairchild F-27.

Sandia Strip, a compacted-earth runway 5,000 feet long and 150 feet wide, was carved out of the desert scrub about a mile from the TTR command post to eliminate the need for using Tonopah Airport. Flight operations began on January 18, 1962, when Nye County airport manager and founder of Mustang Air Service Rick Blakemore touched down in his Cessna 180 to pick up William B. Pepper Jr. and Paul Littell.

Ross Aviation took over from Carco as the charter airlift provider in February 1970. In December 1979, the company replaced the cramped F-27 turboprop with a 70-seat McDonnell Douglas DC-9, offering the first jet service to TTR. Flights typically carried less than 50 passengers, including range personnel and official visitors traveling on a space-available basis four days a week.

Following a 10-hour shift, passengers often slept during the 40-minute flight to Las Vegas. Al Brazda became the first passenger to log one million commuter miles in March 1982, and Dan Tebbs was honored as the 100,000th passenger in July 1984. Beginning in 1973, some Sandia employees with regular job duties at TTR took turns working several extra hours each week as flight attendants on the chartered planes.

The main security gate, on the northern edge of TTR, is down a paved road 20 miles from the nearest highway. This entrance serves as the primary security checkpoint for the entire Tonopah range. Only authorized personnel with appropriate security clearances were permitted access to the test complex. (Gary Selani.)

A Sandia technician drives a pickup truck onto Main Lake after a rainstorm. Most of the year, the lakebeds are dry and hard. Over time, the clay surfaces develop deep cracks that can pose a hazard to drivers. Heavy rains fill the lakebeds with water, softening the clay and allowing the crevices to fill with silt. When dry, the surface is smooth again.

To alleviate the problem of having range workers commute 250 miles by highway from Las Vegas, Sandia arranged to move a number of surplus houses from the Hawthorne Naval Depot to a 10-acre hillside tract just outside the town of Tonopah. In 1983, the Air Force purchased a man camp from Wyoming Oil Shale and moved it to the northern edge of TTR, near the main gate.

By the 1990s, modern, twin-level dormitories provided military and contractor personnel with temporary housing while stationed at TTR. Recreational facilities included a bar, library, game room, weight room, Olympic-size indoor swimming pool, racquetball courts, and a two-lane bowling alley. There was also an athletic track, tennis courts, and softball fields. A new Air Force dining facility offered buffet-style and short order hot food, salads, and sandwiches.

By 1980, the Control Point, formally known as the Range Operations Control Center (ROCC), had grown significantly. One of the most distinctive new features was a four-story control tower building that provided a commanding view of the target areas. The ROCC served as the focal point for coordinating and controlling test activities on the range.

A trio of telemetry receiver antennas at the base of the ROCC provided test conductors and engineers with real-time data for the purpose of monitoring performance of test articles and vehicles while in operation. Afterward, test data were processed into quick-look records for preliminary engineering evaluation or sent to laboratories in New Mexico and California for comprehensive data reduction and archiving.

Range manager Ron Bentley observes a test from the roof of the ROCC in 1992. During his tenure at TTR, he oversaw a staff of fewer than 60 engineers and technicians who maintained and operated a wide variety of systems, often having to modify existing equipment or design new instrumentation as needed to enhance range capabilities.

During testing, assigned test directors such as Joe Dykes, left, and Jim Enlow, seen here in 1992, occupied the control room on the top floor of the four-story ROCC. Large, outward-sloping windows provided a panoramic view of the range. Nearby consoles were occupied by team leaders representing the range's key functional areas.

The Optical Systems Working Group, comprising representatives from military and civilian test ranges across the country, visited TTR in May 1962. Here, they are examining a mobile trailer-mounted ME-16 telescope. The dome at right contains a fixed ME-16 unit, and the tall tower in the background houses a Contraves phototheodolite.

A tracking unit operator gazes through the sighting scope on a mobile ME-16 telescope during a drop test. The long-focal-length lens was equipped with a temperature-correction feature and kept in focus with radar digital range data. Sandia engineers designed and built five ME-16 telescopes at a cost of $100,000 each.

A B-52H drops a B28RI nuclear weapon shape over TTR in 1983. The discarded four-foot pilot chute is visible at lower right, having initiated deployment of a 16-foot ribbon-type extraction chute that will pull out a solid 64-foot parachute. This system decelerated the weapon to allow the delivery aircraft to escape the blast zone.

The unarmed B28RI shape descends to the target beneath a 64-foot parachute. Several versions of the B28 weapon were produced with yields ranging from 70 kilotons to 1.45 megatons. The fuzing mechanism could be set for airburst, ground burst, or delayed detonation. The versatile B28 series was a mainstay of the US nuclear stockpile during the Cold War.

A B-52H based at Mountain Home Air Force Base, Idaho, drops a B53-1 shape over the range. One of the largest US bombs, the B53 was a little over 12 feet long and 50 inches in diameter, weighing more than 8,800 pounds. It was first put into service in 1962 and retired in 1997; all remaining examples were dismantled in 2011.

A trio of parachutes lowers the B53 gently to the ground. This weapon was designed for use against deep underground bunkers such as those used by Soviet leadership during the Cold War. Detonation of a nine-megaton yield at ground level was expected to collapse the earth covering the target. Modern earth-penetrating warheads have made this type obsolete.

The test article lies on the concrete surface of the hard target amidst its collapsed parachutes. The DoD intended to retire the B53 in the 1980s, but 50 units remained in the active stockpile until 1997, when they were rendered obsolete and replaced by the B61-11 ground-penetrating nuclear bomb.

Although the B53 was not known for pinpoint accuracy due to poor ballistic characteristics, this test unit came to rest at the center of the target following release from a B-52F. Operationally, the B53 traded precision for power. Detonated at optimum altitude, it would have produced a fireball approximately three miles in diameter, and the blast would have leveled structures within a nine-mile radius.

OPERATION

Roller Coaster

This is to Certify that

John J. Hess

PARTICIPATED IN THE COMBINED UNITED STATES AND UNITED KINGDOM SCIENTIFIC RESEARCH PROJECT CONDUCTED AT TONOPAH TEST RANGE, NEVADA, SPRING OF 1963

MARK W. NIEMANN COLONEL USA
MILITARY DEPUTY

JAMES L. DICK LT. COLONEL USAF
RESEARCH GROUP DIRECTOR

Operation Roller Coaster, a joint US-British series of weapon safety experiments, subjected actual nuclear warheads to simulated accidents. The tests, named Double Tracks, Clean Slate I, Clean Slate II, and Clean Slate III, produced no nuclear fission, but the high-explosive blasts distributed plutonium and contaminated debris over wide areas. (Author's collection.)

Approximately 81 seconds after detonation, the debris plume from the Clean Slate I shot had risen to more than 1,500 feet. The two black spots above and to the right of the cloud were part of a string of tethered balloons, evenly spaced at 250-foot intervals, that were used by observers to judge cloud height (DOE.)

Radiation safety (Rad-Safe) technicians in anti-contamination gear take soil samples around the perimeter of the Double Tracks site in 1995. Following the Roller Coaster experiments, the contaminated zones were fenced off and marked as prohibited areas and subjected to periodic monitoring. These measures prevented casual access by test range personnel and sequestered larger items of radioactive debris within a controlled area. Rad-Safe monitors discovered that lighter debris in the topsoil was migrating beyond the fence line in the direction of the prevailing winds. Eventually, plans were developed to clean up these areas to the greatest extent possible. The DOE is responsible for remediating sites with legacy contamination resulting from historic nuclear research and testing in Nevada. Completion of site restoration is governed by a legally binding agreement among the DOE, the State of Nevada, and the DoD. (DOE.)

Scotty Afong, at center in the striped shirt, representing DOE Nevada Operations Environmental Restoration Division, poses with five members of the American Indian Rapid Cultural Assessment Team at the Clean Slate II site. The small team of Native Americans (from left to right), Betty Cornelius, Don Cloquet, Gaylene Moose, Maurice Frank, and Richard Arnold, spent several days in September 1996 assessing cultural resources at Project Rollercoaster sites undergoing remediation. (University of Arizona.)

Station 401 on the edge of the Clean Slate III site was one of several solar-powered environmental monitoring units. It was equipped with a continuous air particulate sampler and meteorological station. Particulate specimens collected in 2015 and analyzed by the Radiological Services Laboratory at the University of Nevada, Las Vegas, identified only naturally occurring radionuclides. (NNSA/NV.)

Workers excavate contaminated soil from the Clean Slate II site in 2018. The waste included plutonium debris, which is hazardous only if inhaled or ingested, since the radionuclide emits weak alpha particles that cannot penetrate skin or even a sheet of paper. It does, however, have a half-life of 24,000 years, and small, windborne particles can travel a considerable distance. (NNSA/NV.)

Excavated soil from Clean Slate II is prepared for removal to a waste storage area at the Nevada National Security Site (formerly Nevada Test Site). Remediation of Clean Slate I was completed in October 2016, and Clean Slate II was finished two years later. Cleanup of the Clean Slate III site followed, necessitating the removal of approximately 7,500 cubic yards of contaminated soil and debris. (NNSA/NV.)

Technicians check a flight instrumentation pod made from a converted Mk.43 nuclear bomb casing for a series of tests undertaken by Joint Task Force Two (JTF-2) in 1965. Exercises by JTF-2 sought to identify the most effective methods of finding and striking targets while flying fast and low. Instrumentation specialist Tom Sellers designed the Sandia instrument pod.

A pilot with JTF-2 skims his A-1 Skyraider over Cactus Flat with barely enough altitude to clear one of numerous orange barrels used to mark a winding 150-mile course. Aircraft and crews from the Air Force, Navy, and Marines made approximately 550 flights during the JTF-2 exercises in 1965 and 1966.

An FB-111A drops a B77 test unit to demonstrate a warm-gas roll control system designed to stabilize the weapon's flight path following release. The B77 strategic weapon included improved safety features and a capability for high-speed delivery at extremely low altitudes. From June 1976 through December 1977, the Air Force and Navy conducted 12 drop tests of dummy B77 test units from a variety of aircraft flying at different speeds and altitudes.

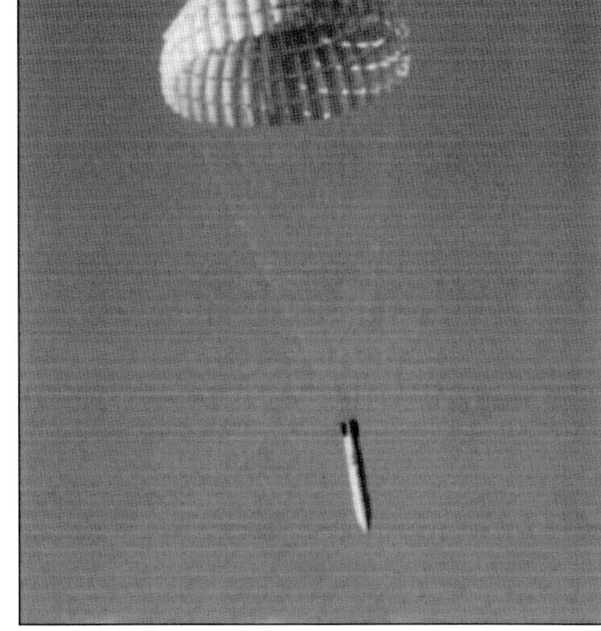

Following shutoff of the gas generator, an instrumented B77 test unit descends toward the target beneath its ring-sail parachute. The 1977 test series successfully demonstrated the feasibility of using a warm-gas device to control roll orientation of the B77 bomb/parachute system and also verified computational models used to predict system performance.

The crew of a B-52G from an operational bombardment squadron performs a laydown delivery of a B77 over the hard target on October 12, 1977. The gas generator kept the weapon within 10 degrees of its ideal angle of attack for the first 3.5 seconds of flight. Excessive costs led to cancellation of B77 development in 1979.

This star-spangled bomb was a fly-around unit for vibration testing of B61 nuclear weapon components. It was used only for captive-carry flights and never dropped. Test team members included, from left to right, Bob Martin, Leland Stone, Dale Buchanan, Jim Lohkamp, Dale Massey, Pete Hernandez, Phil Young, and Larry Johnson. Bill Palmer painted the device in patriotic colors in honor of the US bicentennial in July 1976.

A B61 joint test assembly (JTA) drops away from a B-1B during a 1986 test. A JTA is used for evaluating the functionality and interaction of the weapon's non-nuclear components. First produced in 1966, the B61 series became the most versatile nuclear weapon in the US stockpile. In the first 50 years of service, it was deployed in a dozen variants with different capabilities and safety features.

The B61 JTA descends beneath a 17-foot-diameter parachute that decelerated the 765-pound bomb to an impact velocity of approximately 75 feet per second. The B61 weapons family, some with variable-yield capability, could be delivered for freefall airburst or surface burst, retarded airburst, or in laydown mode. Later models used an improved 24-foot chute.

A Strategic Air Command FB-111A releases a B83 JTA over the hard target on June 6, 1986, with a cluster of three drogue chutes that extract the main chute. The B83 was developed for delivery by tactical and strategic aircraft flying at supersonic speeds and at altitudes as low as 150 feet.

The main B83 chute is extracted during a low-altitude laydown release of the JTA over the hard target. For the purpose of flight testing, selected operational weapons are disassembled and reconfigured into JTAs. All special nuclear material components are replaced with either surrogate materials or instrumentation. These units are typically released by crews and aircraft from the operational command responsible for the system.

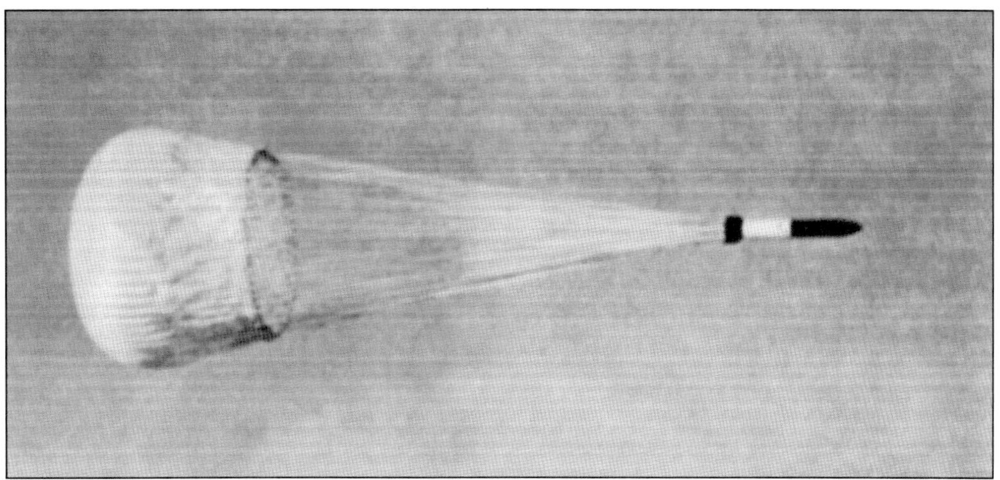

The B83 main parachute was capable of decelerating the 2,400-pound bomb from 0.93 Mach (approximately 1,000 feet per second) to 65 feet per second to mitigate impact forces during laydown. JTA configurations varied from high-fidelity units containing mock nuclear assemblies that recreated, as closely as possible, the mass properties of weapons to fully instrumented units providing detailed information on component and subsystem performance.

Following laydown on the concrete surface, the B83 JTA falls back on its side, and its 46-foot-diameter Kevlar ribbon parachute settles to the ground. After the JTA is recovered, laboratory tests will assess major assemblies and components to evaluate aging trends and anomalous changes at the component and material levels.

A Sandia technician examines a neutron detector near a lakebed target. Some JTA units contain neutron generators, which are components of the weapon's trigger mechanism used to initiate a fission chain reaction. Neutron detectors are positioned in the target area in arrays of 6 to 24, each covering a radius of 375 feet. These devices provide data on JTA component functionality.

Beneath the desert moon, a dry lakebed suggests the surface of an alien world. The playas at Cactus Flat are remnants of an ancient pluvial lake that filled the basin more than 10,000 years ago. As the water dried up, the alkali silt hardened into a series of flat claypans that proved attractive to surveyors seeking a location for the Tonopah ballistics range.

Accompanied by an F-111E chase plane, a B-1B releases a B83 JTA for laydown delivery. The B83 was the first megaton-yield strategic bomb designed for high-speed, low-altitude, delayed-burst delivery. Like the B53, it would have been used to destroy deeply buried targets such as command bunkers. The Cactus Range is visible in the background, with the distinctive profile of Cactus Peak at left. (USAF.)

Two technicians examine a B83 JTA dropped for the stockpile surveillance program. Sandia manages flight test operations for gravity weapons (bombs) to assure compatibility of software and hardware necessary for the interface between the weapon and the delivery aircraft and to assess weapon system functions under realistic delivery conditions.

An F-4D from Edwards Air Force Base, California, drops a B83 JTA in 1983. Several small rocket motors spun the casing to stabilize its flight trajectory immediately following release. Flight testing is used for developmental purposes, to provide proof of weapon reliability and safety, and to demonstrate the effectiveness of the delivery systems.

Following laydown release, a B83 JTA is partially buried in the lakebed surface. This image illustrates the configuration of the Kevlar ribbon decelerator, which was designed to survive opening even at supersonic speeds that would shred a conventional parachute. Gaps between the ribbons allow some air to pass through, reducing stress on the fabric.

An F-4G dropped a Tactical Inertially Guided Extended Range (TIGER II) bomb prototype at TTR on August 25, 1977, to evaluate release and separation characteristics. The TIGER II was a modified B61 retrofitted with a guidance system, canard and rolleron control fins, and a solid-propellant rocket motor to provide standoff delivery capabilities.

Paul Hooper observes the results following a high-velocity impact test of a W61 Earth Penetrating Warhead (EPW) in February 1991. Derived from the B61-7, the W61 EPW was housed inside a single-piece, hardened-steel case that could survive penetration of concrete and low-strength rock. It was proposed as the warhead for the TIGER II but was cancelled in 1992.

During the 1960s, NASA used the airspace over TTR to launch the rocket-powered X-15, a hypersonic research vehicle capable of flying to the edge of space. The X-15 is seen here prior to launch from beneath the wing of a modified B-52, with an Air Force F-100F flying close by as safety chase. The TTR target lakebeds are visible in the background. (USAF.)

From May 1961 through October 1967, three X-15 vehicles were launched 34 times just west of TTR near Mud Lake. Three of these flights resulted in emergency landings on the lakebed. NASA research pilot Jack McKay was injured on November 9, 1962, when one of the vehicle's landing skids collapsed. The second X-15 was rebuilt and flown, eventually setting an unofficial world speed record of 4,520 miles per hour. (NASA.)

From July 1987 through November 1988, the NASA NB-52B was used to drop a parachute test vehicle (PTV) to demonstrate a Sandia-developed improved recovery system for the F-111 escape capsule. This followed two similar series of tests in 1979 and 1982. A fourth series of drop tests took place in 1989. (NASA.)

The PTV was dropped at altitudes varying from about 12,000 to 18,000 feet at increasing airspeeds up to 359 knots as researchers struggled to solve problems of parachute line entanglement and tearing of the chute fabric. This test, on August 16, 1988, used a five-foot-diameter pilot parachute and a 49-foot main chute. (NASA.)

The Nonviolent Explosives Destruct System site, about six miles south of Main Lake, was used for partially or fully contained explosive tests conducted on expendable wooden stands. Tests carried out in the 1970s evaluated the design of shipping and storage containers that would retain the shrapnel, radioactive and toxic debris, and gaseous products that might be produced during the detonation of the high explosives in a nuclear weapon.

Earth penetrator tests may be conducted using a smoothbore, recoilless cannon called a Davis gun that operates on the reaction mass principle. It fires projectiles from both ends of the barrel simultaneously with a reaction mass usually about four times the weight of the penetrator. The mobile gun can be fired at any desired angle and may be transported to areas that have desired soil or rock conditions.

The TTR gun installation provided the means for firing artillery projectiles in standard military gun barrels, such as this 155-millimeter Long Tom, under closely controlled and instrumented conditions. Two custom-designed emplacements were built around standard M158/173 recoil mechanisms that could accommodate barrels up to eight inches in diameter. Unarmed atomic projectiles were tested to assure they could withstand high acceleration loads and spins up to 17,500 revolutions per minute.

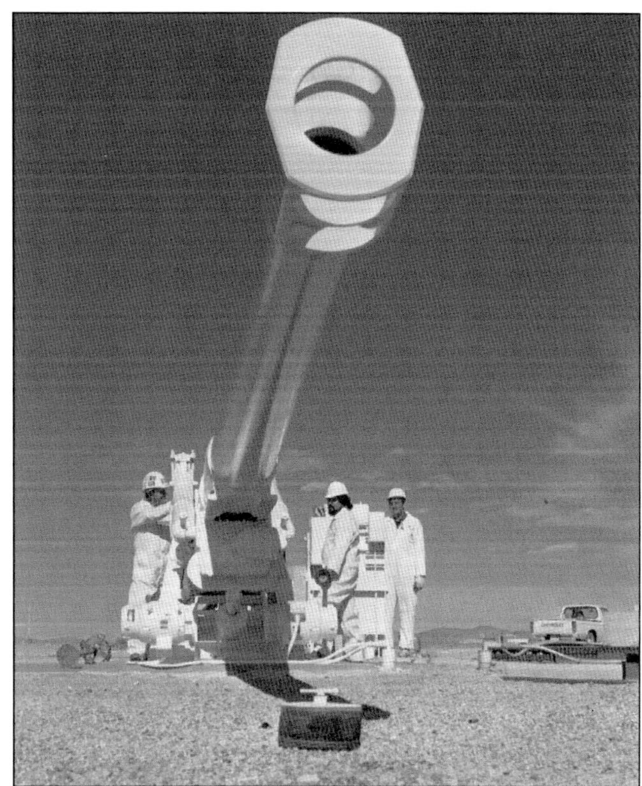

A high-speed camera captures the moment a projectile, instrumented with miniature telemetry systems designed to withstand high acceleration and shock, leaves the barrel of a 155-millimeter howitzer. The second gun was a five-inch, smoothbore cannon with a 40-foot barrel that was capable of firing dart-like projectiles to an altitude of 50 miles. An underground bunker near the gun emplacements provided protection for operating personnel and observers.

Area 9, just east of Main Lake, was built as a rocket test site. Four adjustable-azimuth fixed launch rails are visible at left, and an assembly building can be seen at right. The secure storage igloo in the foreground with the double fence has been used for temporary storage of test articles containing nuclear weapon subassemblies.

Sandia launched this 12-foot-long, unguided, single-stage experimental rocket from TTR in August 1957 to test methods for collecting data at high speeds and altitudes. Subsequent research involved aerodynamics, aeroballistics, and aeroheating studies. The test results contributed to development of a variety of weapons systems and aerospace vehicles. Sandia's George Neun designed the launchers installed at TTR.

Ralph C. Holland of the Sandia Rocket and Ordnance Section inspects a new reinforced concrete blockhouse at Area 9 in October 1964. The new building was constructed to provide onsite launch control and telemetry monitoring of rocket tests. The original blockhouse, at right with a telemetry antenna, was retained for use by observers during firings.

The interior of the control blockhouse was equipped with consoles for the test director, rocket technicians and engineers, and a range safety officer. The outside world was visible only via closed-circuit television screens linked to cameras placed at several locations and through the narrow, blast-proof window on the south wall. A dome light to the right of the viewport flashed if the lightning threat warning system activated.

Two high-altitude diagnostic (HAD) launchers accommodated rocket systems weighing up to 8,000 pounds, and two universal launchers accepted rockets weighting up to 15,350 pounds. Typically, the HAD launcher was used for Nike-Tomahawk and Zap class rockets, while the universal was used for rockets in the Honest John and Strypi classes.

The Area 9 range crew checks a two-stage rocket on its launch rail prior to firing an experimental payload to high altitude. The research rockets designed by Sandia had no internal guidance systems. The launchers and support equipment were selected and modified as needed to assure operational flexibility, safety, and reliability.

A Sandia technician checks the universal launch rail prior to firing an Honest John rocket carrying a special B83 payload. Sometimes it was necessary to loft bomb-type test articles with a rocket in order to attain higher speeds and altitudes than were possible with an airplane. The single-stage, solid-fueled rocket booster was derived from an Army tactical ballistic missile.

A 24-foot-long Sandhawk rocket is poised for launch. A solid-fuel rocket motor could boost the single-stage sounding rocket and a 200-pound payload to an altitude of 110 miles above Earth's surface. TTR rocket shots were used for research involving parachute development, rain erosion, vehicle stabilization, weapon fuzing, reentry vehicle performance, high-altitude radio-chemistry, and chaff dispensers.

An F-4J from the Naval Air Test Center prepares to release a Pedro-Recruit rocket carrying the Fighter-Launched Advanced Materials Experiment (FLAME). The purpose of the experiment, sponsored by the Defense Nuclear Agency, was to test missile nose cone materials at reentry dynamic pressures and speeds of around 13,000 feet per second. The nose cones were recovered by parachute for later study.

An unguided M26 rocket leaves the launch rail for a bomblet dispersal test. Designed for use with the M270 Multiple Launch Rocket System (MLRS), the M26 was armed with 644 dual-purpose anti-personnel/anti-materiel grenades. The rocket's warhead dispensed these submunitions widely over the target area, where they detonated on impact. First employed during Operation Desert Storm in 1991, the MLRS/M26 system acquired the nickname "steel rain."

A two-stage Terrier-derivative booster lofts a test article off the back of a mobile rocket launch platform built from a modified Army M53 two-and-a-half-ton truck chassis. From the late 1950s into the 1970s, Sandia high-altitude research rockets were used to develop missile warhead reentry vehicles for intercontinental ballistic missiles. A variety of experimental nose cones carried diagnostic packages aloft for investigations of ablative heat-shield materials, anti-radiation hardening of sensitive electronic components, and methods for reducing the warhead's radar signature to prevent intercept by hostile air defenses. Materials researchers tested various combinations of carbon-carbon and carbon-phenolic compounds by accelerating recoverable nose cones up to 11,000 feet per second to evaluate resistance to atmospheric heating, ablation, and rain erosion. Sandia scientists also studied reentry effects on telemetry systems, proximity fuzes, and other internal components exposed to environmental conditions at the edge of space.

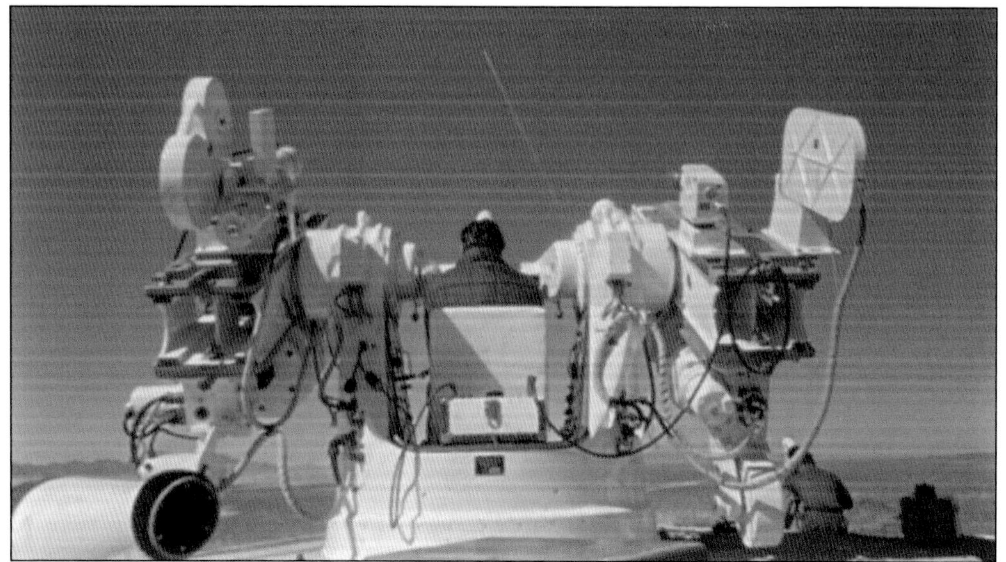

Sandia photographers document a rocket launch from one of several remote sites using a variety of equipment, including 12-inch-aperture, 60-inch-focal-length telescopes. This SM-30 mobile tracking unit was equipped with several types of motion picture camera attached to high-performance mounts with a 50-degree-per-second slew rate. Another photographer using a tripod-mounted camera with telephoto lens is visible at lower right.

Air Force and DOE environmental management specialists examine a partially buried rocket at TTR in 2013. While its origin and timeframe were unknown, range personnel had reported seeing it since the mid-1980s. Following inspections that found the rocket to be free of explosive hazards, the DOE Nevada Field Office made plans to remove it, a task complicated by its location within the Clean Slate III contaminated zone. (DOE.)

A rare sight, the TTR Control Point is surrounded by snow. The range is on a flat plain with an elevation around 5,700 feet and surrounded by mountains. The climate is typically mild and dry but given to seasonal temperature changes ranging from 102 degrees in summer to minus 24 degrees in winter.

A research and development tracking telescope records event data with a high-speed camera and provides real-time video for situational awareness. The instrument can be slaved to tracking radar systems for target acquisition and to provide ranging information for camera focus. The universal mount can accommodate up to two additional customer-provided sensors or act as a testbed for new imagers and auto-tracker development.

A technician deploys a remote optical tracking system. Previously, the operator was required to man the mount in the field. Sandia's 21st-century range upgrade included optical sensors that allowed for remote operation from the ROCC using a digital console and joystick. Operators linked via headsets could coordinate with the mission controller and with each other.

Optical calibration panels with checkerboard patterns were placed at various locations around the range. Prior to a test, camera and telescope operators used these panels to adjust the focus on their equipment. Still photographs and motion pictures were valuable for post-test engineering evaluation of test results as well as for archival purposes.

A photometrics technician calibrates mobile cinetheodolite equipment before returning it to the field. Cinetheodolites track time, space, and position information, recording the angular position from the mount location to the test object. By triangulating the vectors generated by three or more units, a cinetheodolite operator can determine the test article's geospatial position to within one cubic meter.

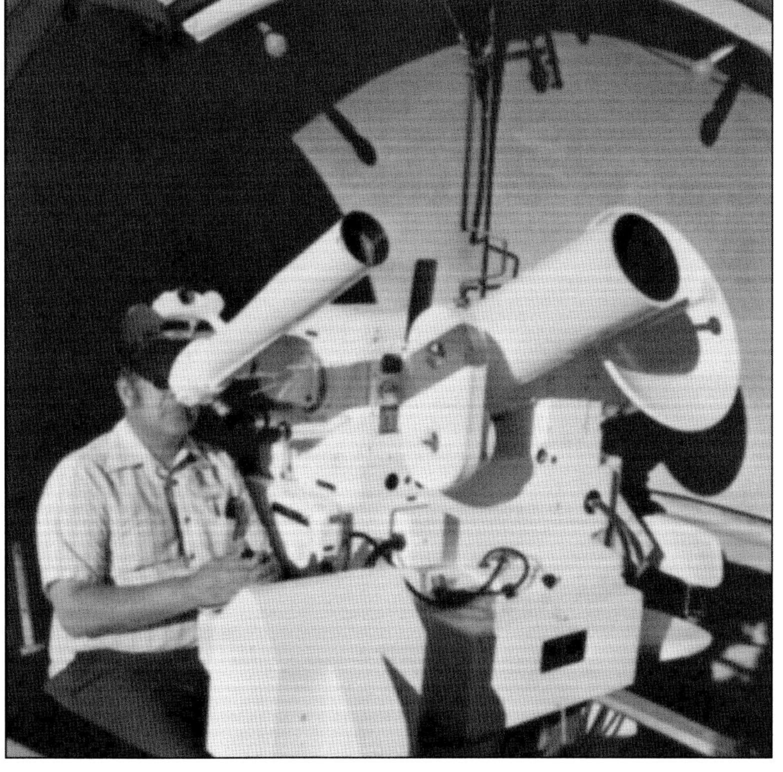

An operator uses a mobile cinetheodolite equipped with ranging radar to take motion pictures of a test article in flight. The device annotates the film or digital imagery with precise time-space-position data. This is an older model; newer tracking units are remotely operated from the ROCC.

Perched at the crest of Radar Hill, 700 feet above the valley floor, the MPS-25 monopulse G-band tracking system had an effective range of 500 miles. The one-megawatt radar with its 12-foot parabolic dish antenna cost more than $2 million when it was purchased around 1960. Its primary function was aircraft guidance and control during test operations.

A photometrics technician checks a bore-sighted optical system slaved to the MPS-25 radar dish. Telescopic cameras were mounted on most TTR tracking equipment to collect imagery for documentary and engineering purposes. Video was not only recorded but also transmitted in real time to the operations center for display in the control room and plotting room.

A B-2 drops a B83 JTA over TTR. In order to survive delivery from fast, low-flying aircraft, the bomb had to be slowed to about 60 miles per hour with a rugged parachute system. A high-strength steel casing and internal shock absorbers ensured sensitive internal components of the nuclear fuzing and firing mechanism would withstand impact forces as the weapon struck such target complexes as railroad marshaling yards or steel production plants. After coming to rest, the electrical system would have to continue to function reliably so as to provide safe escape time for the delivery aircraft. Gary Beeler, who in 1981 headed the Sandia B83 structural design team, described the inherent challenge of building such a device as akin to "stopping a compact car going 60 miles per hour in six inches and expecting the radio to still work."

An F-111F of the 431st Test and Evaluation Squadron at McClellan Air Force Base, California, dropped the first GBU-28 at TTR in February 1991. The weapon, more than nine feet long and weighing 4,700 pounds, was the result of a crash effort to develop a non-nuclear bunker buster during Operation Desert Storm. (USAF.)

During its first test, the GBU-28 buried itself too deep for recovery. The bomb design was approved on February 13, 1991. Development, testing, and deployment all took place within two weeks. Three days after the February 24 test drop at TTR, the first operational combat employment of the GBU-28 destroyed an Iraqi command and control bunker. (USAF.)

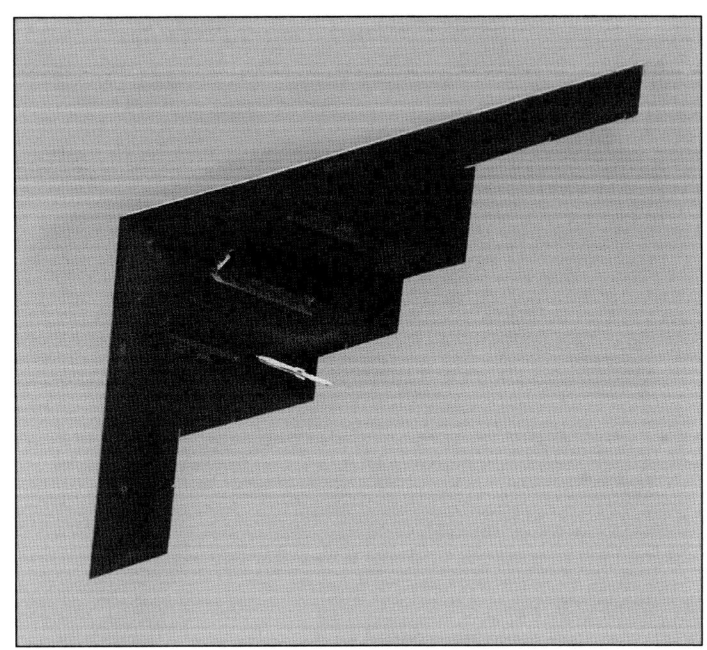

An operational B-2 from Whiteman Air Force Base, Missouri, drops a B61-7 JTA as part of the stockpile surveillance program. In the multi-step operation, technicians at Pantex in Amarillo, Texas, removed nuclear components from a war reserve bomb, rendering it incapable of producing a nuclear yield. Sandia added special instrumentation and sensors to monitor the performance of numerous components during flight test to determine whether the weapon functioned as designed.

Following a successful drop, a B61-7 JTA is examined prior to recovery from the concrete surface of the hard target. Note the heavily armed Cadillac Gage Peacekeeper security vehicle in the background. The Peacekeeper was built from a modified Dodge 1.25-ton four-wheel-drive truck chassis, with a body fabricated from specially engineered hardened armor plate that encompassed the entire vehicle, including the cabin floor.

A B-2 releases an AGM-158 Joint Air-to-Surface Standoff Missile (JASSM), a stealthy, long-range, conventional, air-launched weapon with precision guidance. Integrated with a variety of delivery platforms, the JASSM was designed to destroy high-value, well-defended, and fortified targets from standoff distances that would keep aircrews well out of danger from hostile air defense systems. (USAF.)

A JASSM test article passes through the front window of a concrete target bunker. A 2,000-pound-class weapon with a penetrator/blast-fragmentation warhead, the JASSM was equipped with precision routing and guidance. It was capable of striking targets in adverse weather, day or night, using a state-of-the-art infrared seeker in addition to anti-jam GPS to find a specific aimpoint on the target. (USAF.)

During JASSM operational test OT-5, the missile targeted a trailer topped with a modified M-33 anti-aircraft fire control radar. Trailer F-19, also known as "Mustang," had been a fixture at TTR for several decades. The earthen berm surrounding the trailer was part of a simulated Soviet-type surface-to-air missile launch site located about 1,700 feet east of Antelope Lake.

Communications electromechanical technologist Mark Gonzales checks fiber optic cables at a remote station. Because TTR covers nearly 300 square miles, reliable communications are essential to ensure the safety of range personnel and visitors and for coordination of test and maintenance activities. Fiber optic cables provide access to broadband communications such as video feeds and high-speed data networks.

Bob Beasley, left, and Al Brazda work in the range telemetry center around 1971. This central station in the ROCC building, along with mobile telemetry stations at remote sites, recorded a wide variety of data transmitted from test articles. Information was immediately transmitted to test controllers and also recorded for later analysis.

Test director Bob Sherwood, left, and Henry Stuckert scan the horizon from atop the large telemetry-receiving antenna in front of the TTR command post. The master ground station in the ROCC served as the controlling element for all telemetry functions at TTR, providing reception, recording, real-time evaluation, and post-test data playback.

A volcanic knob about five miles southwest of Antelope Lake was flattened to make room for radar, telemetry, and optical tracking equipment. The establishment of remote stations like this assured coverage of critical areas of test vehicle trajectories. Tracking data were relayed to the control center via microwave link.

A telemetry specialist monitors incoming data during a drop test. Data needed to make real-time go/no-go decisions have been displayed in a variety of ways at TTR: on analog meters, oscillographs or strip charts, oscilloscopes, spectrum analyzers, computer printouts, and CRT screens with alphanumeric displays. Obsolete systems have been upgraded with modern digital displays.

The operations center control room is a hive of activity during a test in which a B-2 will drop a JTA over Main Lake Target. The test director and systems monitors are intently focused on their display consoles, while observers on the outdoor balcony search the skies with binoculars.

From its location on the top floor of the ROCC, the operations control room commands a 360-degree view of the range. Computer monitors display charts that track all air traffic over TTR and the surrounding Nevada Test and Training Range. Telemetry readouts provide the status of test articles and delivery aircraft. The surrounding work consoles are used to control and coordinate test functions.

Silhouetted against the dawn sky, an F-15D accelerates at full afterburner prior to dropping a B61 JTA over the range. The mission was part of a joint Sandia–Air Force partnership to execute a series of development flight tests and compatibility tests involving three types of aircraft. Missions using F-15 and F-16 aircraft were staged out of Nellis Air Force Base, while B-2 missions operated from Edwards Air Force Base.

Following a winter test, Sandia personnel excavate a B61 JTA from the soggy lakebed and hoist it with a crane. Though the B61 was introduced into the stockpile more than half a century ago, continuing tests support the B61 Life Extension Program (LEP), which allows scientists and engineers to address the aging of nuclear weapon components. Some components are requalified, while others are remanufactured or redesigned using modern technology.

The crew of a UH-1 helicopter prepares to drop a B61 JTA for a radar test drop in 2013. The bomb, approximately 12 feet long and weighing about 825 pounds, will be scanned using several radar frequencies and the data analyzed for use in tracking future drops from bomber and fighter aircraft.

The range control position in the ROCC is primarily responsible for monitoring the local airspace and providing test status information to test operations personnel in the field. The range controller monitors the Test and Evaluation Command and Control System to follow the test aircraft's flight path, location status, countdown to camera activation, and test unit release point.

The B61 LEP continued in 2012 with design and development of the B61-12, which was programmed to replace existing B61-3, -4, -7, and -10 bombs in the stockpile. This called for refurbishment of nuclear and non-nuclear components to extend the bomb's service life while improving safety, security, and reliability. Here, a B61-12 JTA is released from an F-15E on July 1, 2015. (NNSA/NV.)

The moon hangs low in the sky as the operator of a fixed ME-16 telescope readies his equipment. Tracking scopes provide very clear high-resolution still and motion picture images for use in post-test analysis and engineering data reduction. Optical trackers are located around the target area and along the flight path of the delivery aircraft.

Range personnel attend a preflight mission briefing at the ROCC. Every test operation is subject to extensive planning and preparation. Every detail must be coordinated among the participating government agencies and military services using the range in order to maintain safety and security and ensure the greatest chance of a successful outcome.

Prior to aerial tests, weather balloons may be released to collect atmospheric data. Knowing the conditions at various altitudes helps engineers correlate any anomalies in test data that could be weather related. The balloons are used for determining upper-atmosphere wind speeds and direction. When equipped with radiosondes, they also measure temperature, humidity, and pressure and can be tracked by any of the range tracking radars.

The test director is responsible for control and coordination of test-related activities during preliminary planning, execution, and post-test operations and is the single point of contact during any given test operation. The test director participates in safety planning and monitors operations to assure all flight-safety criteria are met.

A technician operates a high-power telescope remotely from a control station in the ROCC. Optical instruments using a 117-inch Newtonian lens can record imagery without distortion at a distance of five miles. Focus is controlled using tracking radars slaved to the scope to provide target acquisition and ranging information.

Sandia test operations personnel monitor a JTA drop over the range. The operations center houses mission-critical systems and specialists who coordinate test activities. More than three dozen electronic displays provide detailed tracking information along with multiple views of test events as they occur. A unified communications server integrates fixed radio and telephone systems to ensure effective command and control, situational awareness, and safety.

Sandia telemetry systems technologist Mark Skobel adjusts patch cables on a panel in the telemetry ground station at the ROCC. Telemetry at TTR consists primarily of equipment and antenna systems within the Control Point area and at several remote sites around the range to capture and record vital event data during tests.

The track control operator coordinates all optical tracking activities. This control station provides readiness status information for radar and optical systems to the test director. The track control operator monitors test operations, sends signals to synchronize camera start and stop times, and uses streaming video from radar and optical trackers to verify ranging data.

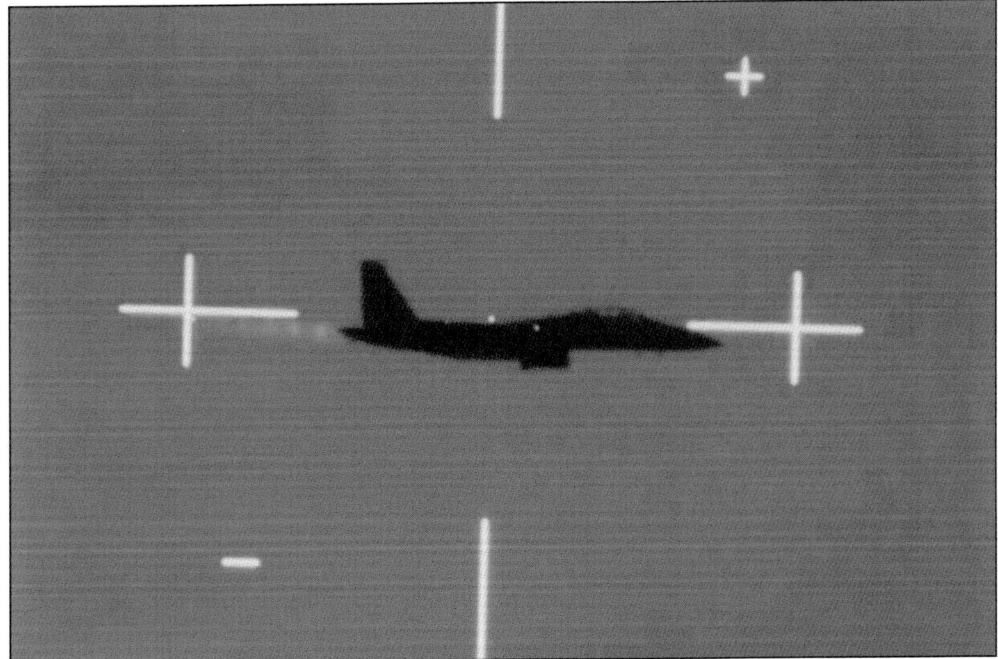

A cinetheodolite provides a clear image of a distant F-15D during testing of a B61-12 JTA. This instrument uses 21-bit optical encoders to record the angular position of the optical unit relative to the test object, allowing for precise triangulation. The mount is equipped with a digital camera for image capture, a computer to record data, and a fiber-optic data-transfer system.

An F-15D from the 48th Fighter Wing drops a B61-12 JTA. Over the decades, numerous modifications were made to increase the safety and reliability of the B61 family of weapons. The -12 mod was designed to consolidate and replace most of the previous variants. Improvements to the bomb's tail assembly and internal systems necessitated compatibility testing with all relevant delivery platforms. (USAF.)

A motion picture photographer documents the recovery of a JTA from the target. Note that the nose cone, damaged upon impact, has been taped to secure any loose items. The expended test unit will be disassembled and examined by qualified nuclear weaponeers before being packaged and shipped back to the sponsoring organization.

Sandia personnel wait to place the B61 JTA into the secure storage igloo in Area 9. Parts from recovered JTAs may be used as many as three times if the mock weapon is dropped using a parachute. At their fourth use, the parts may be installed on test units destined for non-retarded drops that result in total destruction of the device.

A B61 JTA is disassembled following a test drop to improve understanding of aging weapon component reliability. Test results are carefully studied to unearth clues about potential defects and how a weapon's performance changes over time. These efforts ultimately help ensure the safety, security, and performance of the US nuclear deterrent.

A B61 JTA drops from the left wing of an F-16; a second awaits release from the airplane's right wing. These test units were assembled from components produced by the Kansas City National Security Campus, Kansas City, Missouri; Sandia National Laboratories, Albuquerque, New Mexico; and Los Alamos National Laboratory, Los Alamos, New Mexico.

This MPS-36 C-band radar was placed on one of the highest peaks at TTR for maximum coverage and to minimize the effects of ground clutter. This one-megawatt, pulse-Doppler radar was designed to have the capability to track a beacon-equipped vehicle as far away as 31,000 miles or skin-track an object as small as a football from a distance of 87 miles.

This eight-foot-diameter X-band radar is one of two used at TTR for controlling air traffic over the test range. The shorter wavelengths produced within the X band allow for acquisition of higher-resolution radar imagery for target identification and discrimination. All radar systems at TTR are capable of tracking targets both with and without beacons.

A TTR radar operator surveys his console in the operations center. During flight test operations, radar data output drives the plotting boards and graphic displays used by test controllers and provides time-space-position information to the computer for analysis with real-time trajectory-prediction programs. This information assures acquisition of the target by all range instrumentation and optical systems.

Following Operation Desert Storm, the B61-11 was developed to ensure a capability to hold selected deeply buried targets at risk. This B61-11 certification drop from a B-2 took place on November 20, 1996. Derived from the B61-7, the B61-11 incorporated the same earth-penetrating case forgings used on the cancelled W61 EPW. No changes were made to the B61-7 electrical or nuclear systems. (USAF.)

Like many of its predecessors, the B61-11 employed spin motors for ballistic stability during flight toward the target. Penetration tests with functional warhead electrical-system components and simulated nuclear assemblies were conducted at different impact velocities and soil conditions to demonstrate component and system survivability. Following additional flight tests, the B61-11 entered the US nuclear stockpile in 1997.

In this test, the warhead of a B61-11 penetrated a foot of concrete over hard earth and came to rest almost nine feet below the surface. Subsequent tests with an improved penetrator went even deeper. Sandia weaponeers retrofitted the B61-7 with a high-strength steel case, removed the parachute, and installed ballast on the aft end. Shortening the earth-penetrating nose cone and installing a plastic aeroshell ensured the weapon had exterior geometry identical to that of the B61-7.

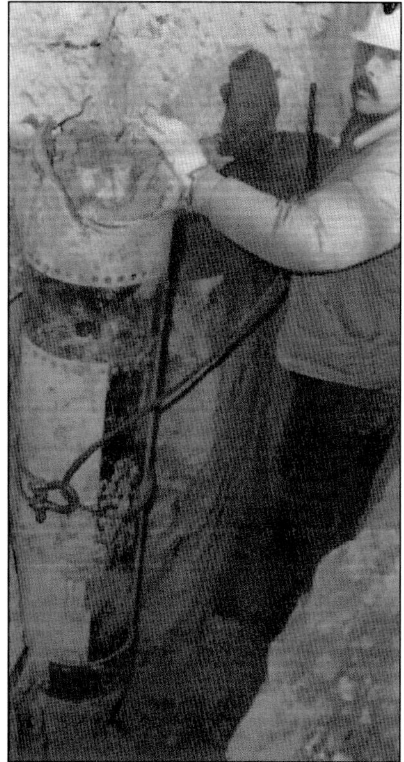

A worker examines the excavated B61-11 penetrator deep beneath the target surface. Sandia performed tests of several designs to assess the stress on the weapon's internal components and the ability of the steel casing to withstand high-speed impacts in sand, soil, clay, rock, concrete, and permafrost. The final configuration drew heavily upon the previously cancelled W61 earth-penetrator design.

Recovery of deeply buried objects, such as this B61-11 test article, necessitated the use of steel platforms that allowed a cylindrical collar to be placed atop the excavation to prevent cave-ins. A total of 25 full-scale drop B61-11 tests were performed in 1996 and 1998, mostly at TTR. Penetrator testing in frozen soil took place at a range in Alaska.

Posing like fishermen with a prize catch, Jim Keagy and Pam Schorzman display a recovered B61-11 test unit. In April 2011, the NNSA and Air Force Global Strike Command tested a B61-11 JTA instrumented to collect data for use in developing a reliability model of the weapon. The JTA was dropped from a B-2A assigned to the 509th Bomb Wing, Whiteman Air Force Base.

A B61 JTA plummets toward a target at TTR during Weapons Systems Evaluation Program (WSEP) flight tests. These flights are part of DOE and DoD surveillance testing of the enduring stockpile and not a test of new weapons or weapon components. The B61 JTA flight test program evaluates weapons reliability, safety, and use-control features. The primary purpose is the timely detection and correction of problems in stockpile hardware, ensuring that materials conform to design and reliability requirements. Goals include verification of weapon system function (less the nuclear assembly) and demonstration of continuing compatibility among subsystems using flight testing and the most realistic environmental conditions. Each JTA retains as many war reserve components as possible, including portions of the explosive package, but no JTA configuration is capable of nuclear detonation. As of 2020, there were five operational B61 variants in the US stockpile. The B61-3/-4/-10 mods are intended for delivery by tactical aircraft such as the F-15, F-16, and B-1. The B61-7/-11 mods are designated for delivery by strategic bomber aircraft such as the B-2 and B-21.

An F-16D from Eglin Air Force Base, Florida, releases a B61-12 developmental test unit at TTR in 2018. Along with the F-15E and F-16C/D series fighters, the B61-12 was certified for delivery from the B-2 strategic bomber and the F-35 fifth-generation fighter. Compatibility testing was essential to extending the B61 weapon's service life by at least 20 years and improving its safety, security, and effectiveness.

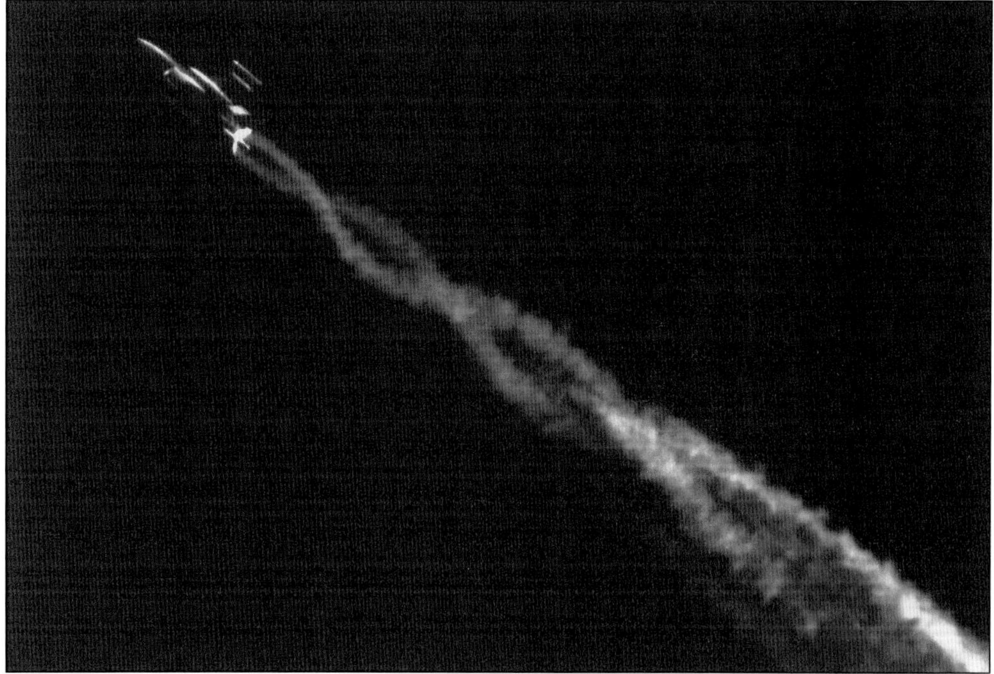

Immediately following release from an F-16D, the B61-12's spin motor ignites, stabilizing the bomb's trajectory. The mod 12 version of the bomb is equipped with a special tail kit for guided flight to the target. Design features including adjustable yield and precision targeting allow the production B61-12 to be capable of earth-penetrating bunker-buster attack, low-yield and high-yield detonation, above-surface burst, or ground burst, as required.

In February 1980, Sandia tested a multi-fuze configuration on an Honest John rocket. At the time, the Army's Harry Diamond Laboratories was developing a fuzing system for what became the M270 MLRS, and the hydra-headed nose tip developed by Sandia made it possible to test five separate fuzes on a single rocket.

TTR heavy equipment manager Cecil Lang, left, looks on as Sandia excess property procurement specialist Louise Bland sits atop one of eight Sergeant York automated air-defense guns she acquired for the range from the Army in 1988. With their sophisticated radar systems, the mobile guns were considered ideal for use as trackers and camera platforms, with possible applications for range security.

Extremely high security at the weapon storage igloo protects test assemblies with sensitive components. The concrete bunker is surrounded by steel "hedgehog" vehicle barricades and a double fence topped with barbed wire and separated by no-man's land. A cadre of highly trained and equipped paramilitary security personnel ensures protection of facilities, range assets, and special nuclear materials.

The TTR security force acquired a few Chenowth Scorpion desert patrol vehicles for range reconnaissance. These were produced in the 1980s for the Naval Special Warfare Group, Army Special Forces, and British Special Air Service. The lightweight, off-road vehicle could attain speeds of up to 60 miles per hour and was armed with a Browning .50-caliber heavy machine gun and an M60 .30-caliber general-purpose machine gun.

Two

Red Eagles

In November 2006, following nearly three decades of secrecy, the Air Force publicly acknowledged operating foreign military aircraft at TTR from 1977 through 1988. Known as Constant Peg, the program pitted Air Force, Navy, and Marine Corps aircrews against Soviet-designed fighters in realistic mock combat exercises to train American pilots in how to defeat the kind of adversary aircraft they would most likely face in any future war. (USAF.)

Sandia Strip was selected to be the base for Constant Peg. Originally just a bare field, it was not even equipped with runway lights until 1969. The airstrip was paved and extended to 6,600 feet with a 1,500-foot overrun in 1970 and provided with instrument-approach equipment the following year. The runway was completely repaved in 1976 with a strengthened all-weather surface at a cost of $540,000.

In May 1978, the deputy secretary of defense approved $7 million to fund phase one construction of new airfield and support facilities at TTR for the organization carrying out Constant Peg, the 4477th Test and Evaluation Flight, better known as the Red Eagles. Initial construction included a maintenance hangar, parking apron, taxiway, propane tank, a few permanent outbuildings, and 16 mobile homes to serve as personnel accommodations. (USAF.)

Sandia Strip was extended to 10,000 feet with a 1,000-foot overrun on each end and equipped with two arresting barriers and upgraded systems for navigation and instrument landings. Phase two construction, which began on September 16, 1980, included expansion of the parking apron and construction of a taxiway, fuel and water storage tanks, a dining hall, a warehouse, support utilities, and 42,000 square feet of hangar space. (USAF.)

The 4477th TEF compound was essentially ready by late 1979. The large and small U-shaped groups of trailers at lower right, dubbed the "Indian Village," served as temporary barracks for the Red Eagles until the man camp facility became available. The oval "rubber duck" shelter to the right of the hangars was used for supply storage. (USAF.)

The airfield and Red Eagles facilities are visible behind the Sandia command post and operations center. Phase two construction costs totaled approximately $18 million. Holmes and Narver (H&N) of Orange, California, was responsible for architectural and engineering design for the airfield facilities; REECo handled the actual construction. To conceal the true nature of the facility, H&N dubbed it the Tonopah Integrated Air Defense System project.

Vehicle mechanic Billy Lightfoot holds up a sign by the doorway of the 4477th TEF operations trailer around 1979. This spartan facility was eventually replaced with an actual building as airfield construction continued over several years. The Jeep at left is one of several vehicles Lightfoot scrounged and restored. (REAA.)

Completion of phase two marked the transition of the TTR airfield from a bare base to a standard Air Force base. The construction effort greatly increased the amount of hangar space and administrative facilities and gave the airfield a dedicated control tower for the first time. (Gabe Zeifman.)

Men of the 4477th TEF pose in front of a Navy QF-86F, one of many aircraft to visit TTR after the facility was complete but before the start of MiG flight operations. From left to right are Lt. Comdr. Charles "Heater" Heatley, Capt. Bud "Chops" Horan, Capt. Karl "Harpo" Whittenberg, Maj. Gerry "Huffer" Huff, Capt. Dave "Marshall" McCloud, Lt. Comdr. Tom "Squid" Morgenfeld, and Maj. Don "Devil" Muller. (REAA.)

A Navy F-14A is parked by the refueling pad in front of the 4477th TEF hangars during a time that came to be known as the "period of tactical deception." The Red Eagles hosted as many different types of aircraft as possible, timing visits to coincide with Russian spy satellite overhead times in order to confuse adversary intelligence analysts as to the nature of activities at the new airfield. (REAA.)

In July 1979, Lt. Col. Gaillard Peck led a flight of eight jet fighters to TTR, six MiG-21s and two MiG-17s. These airplanes had been acquired from foreign sources, and most were in poor condition. Each airframe underwent meticulous repair and restoration to flyable condition. The innovative and talented Red Eagles maintenance crews became the true heroes of the Constant Peg program. (USAF.)

The MiG-17 was highly maneuverable but had a propensity to snap into a spin. A skilled pilot could use this characteristic to tactical advantage, but it could also prove deadly, as demonstrated when a loss-of-control mishap took the life of Navy lieutenant Hugh Brown. MiG-17 flight operations ended in 1982 after an engine problem prompted Capt. Mark Postai to crash land in the desert immediately after takeoff. He escaped uninjured. (REAA.)

A MiG-21 taxies in from the runway. By 1985, the Red Eagles had 17 flyable MiG-21s operating from TTR. One was lost due to engine failure in June 1987, but the pilot ejected safely. Though less maneuverable than the MiG-17, the MiG-21 was a formidable adversary in air-to-air engagements. (REAA.)

A MiG-17 leads a four-ship formation trailed by a MiG-21. The two accompanying jets are F-5E fighters from the 64th Aggressor Squadron at Nellis Air Force Base. The Aggressors used the F-5E to simulate MiG-21 performance characteristics, as well as Soviet tactics, in mock aerial combat during annual Red Flag training exercises. (USAF.)

A MiG-21 banks majestically over TTR. Pedro Lake Target and the curving arc of Browne's Lake Road are visible at lower right. The sleek lines and elegant simplicity of the delta-winged MiG-21 are readily apparent from this angle. The airplane was technologically crude by American standards, but rugged and reliable. (USAF.)

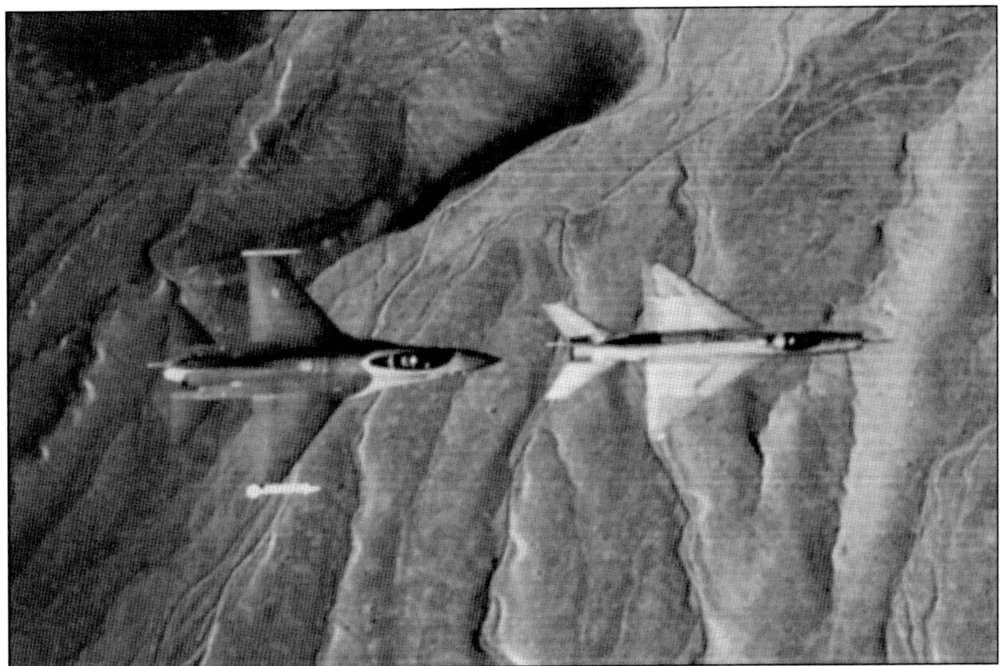

An F-16A flies in close trail behind a MiG-21 over the Nevada Test and Training Range. One of the most agile US fighters, the F-16 was designed to execute nine-g turns and accelerate to speeds above Mach 2. An older aircraft by about two decades, the MiG-21 was smaller, lighter, and capable of attaining Mach 2 dash speeds, making it a formidable opponent. (USAF.)

Sporting a Communist red star insignia on its tail, the MiG-21 looks incongruous parked beside the American flag waving proudly on its pole beside the taxiway. Red Eagles jets displayed a wide variety of paint schemes representing those used by Communist air forces and those of Soviet client states and allies. (USAF.)

Side by side on the ramp are a MiG-21, left, and its Chinese doppelganger, a Chengdu J-7. The canopy hinge location was the only noticeable external difference. Produced by the Shenyang Aircraft Factory, the J-7 was nearly identical to the Russian MiG-21F-13. Though slightly heavier and less maneuverable, the J-7 had a structurally stronger fuselage. (USAF.)

A two-ship MiG-21 sortie heads out to the range for mock combat exercises. In May 1980, the 4477th TEF was redesignated the 4477th Test and Evaluation Squadron. Upgrade to squadron status reflected the unit's growing importance. In August, the 4477th TES was placed under responsibility of the deputy commander, tactics and test, 57th Fighter Weapons Wing. (USAF.)

MiG-21 and J-7 variants lining the TTR ramp sport a diverse medley of paint schemes. By 1985, the Red Eagles were operating 17 of these aircraft, accounting for approximately 63 percent of the squadron's assets. One of the J-7s crashed in June 1987 during flameout approach to the runway following engine failure. Capt. Rick Cazessus ejected. (USAF.)

An overseas scavenging trip yielded two self-propelled Russian aircraft-starting trucks, variations of the venerable Gaz-63 4x4 utility vehicle. These relics were in terrible shape, but the skilled mechanics of the 4477th TES restored them and greatly improved their efficiency on the flight line. In keeping with the squadron's Russian theme, the two vehicles were nicknamed "Ivan" and "Natasha." (USAF.)

"Red 84" taxies past the control tower. In keeping with Soviet practice, each of the Red Eagles planes had a "bort number" painted on the side of the forward fuselage. These tactical markings took the place of a standard tail number. Maintenance crews of the 4477th TES knew each aircraft by a small number painted on the nose gear door, in this case number 11. (USAF.)

"Red 69" touches down on the runway following a successful mission. During nearly a decade of operations, the Red Eagles flew 15,500 sorties and exposed 5,930 Air Force, Navy, and Marine Corps flyers to realistic aerial combat against actual Soviet-type military hardware. Results of these training exercises were distributed to front-line combat forces. (USAF.)

An instructor from the USAF Fighter Weapons School at Nellis Air Force Base is checked out in the cramped cockpit of a J-7. The school was created to provide advanced training in weapons and tactics employment to officers of the combat air forces. These officers would then serve as advisors to military and civilian defense leaders and act as an institutional reservoir of tactical and operational knowledge. (USAF.)

This is the view looking down the TTR runway through the MiG-21's head-up display. The tiny circle in the center is the gun-sighting reticle. Degraded forward visibility through the sight-combining glass, bulletproof glass slab, and forward windscreen limited visual target detection. Rearward visibility was restricted by the seat headrest, narrow canopy, and aircraft structure. (USAF.)

The Red Eagles played a vital role in US efforts to gain an advantage against Communist adversaries during the Cold War. In addition, the benefits of Constant Peg training sorties led to success in aerial engagements between US F-14 Tomcats and Libyan Su-22 and MiG-23 fighters over the Gulf of Sidra in 1981 and 1989, as well as during Desert Storm and subsequent operations in Iraq and Kosovo. (USAF.)

Personnel of the 4477th TES pose in front of an F-5E on June 6, 1980, following a change-of-command ceremony in which Lt. Col. Earl Henderson relinquished command of the unit to Lt. Col. Tom Gibbs. The officers, kneeling in front, included two Navy exchange pilots. The enlisted maintenance crewmen are standing behind them, wearing pristine white jumpsuits. (USAF.)

Brig. Gen. Charles J. Cunningham Jr., commander of the 57th Fighter Weapons Wing, presents Air Force Commendation Medals to Red Eagles enlisted personnel (from left to right) Bill McHenry, crew chief; Gary Lewallen, operations; and Ben Galloway, aerospace ground equipment specialist. A special exemption from AFR 35-10 Dress and Grooming Standards permitted the obviously non-regulation haircuts. (USAF.)

Crew chief Tommy Karnes smiles for the camera, perhaps pleased that blue jeans and cowboy hats were often the Red Eagles' uniform of the day. In the early years of operation, security requirements mandated that because of the amount of time they spent in downtown Tonopah, the men needed to blend in with the local population. (REAA.)

One of the first ground transportation vehicles assigned to the Red Eagles was a Kenworth tractor truck capable of 18-wheel trailer operations and nicknamed the "K-Whopper." The driver's cab was painted dark blue with Air Force markings. Lt. Comdr. Charles "Heater" Heatley cleverly framed this scene to create the illusion that its 40-foot flatbed trailer could carry a C-141A cargo transport. (REAA.)

Bobby Ellis, far left, poses with eight of his Red Eagles maintenance crew in front of the K-Whopper. One of the hangars, with the door to the maintenance shop, is visible in the background. Aircraft maintenance for the MiGs was accomplished without blueprints or technical manuals using scrounged, rebuilt, or reverse-engineered parts. (REAA.)

The Red Eagles fleet was augmented by five T-38A two-seat trainers that were used for safety chase when new pilots were flying the single-seat MiGs for the first few times; no MiG trainers were available. Painted in Soviet-style camouflage like Aggressor aircraft at Nellis, the T-38s also provided cover for the 4477th as well as a platform for proficiency flying when the MiGs were unavailable. (USAF.)

Phase three construction added new hangars and airfield improvements, including fire stations, additional fuel storage, and warehousing, at a cost of $79 million. Most of these facilities were not built for the Red Eagles but for another organization that would soon move into TTR. Around this time, the Red Eagles personnel moved their overnight quarters to the man camp and adopted Air Force grooming standards. (Gabe Zeifman.)

Col. John "Jack" Manclark took command of the 4477th TES in January 1986 and oversaw the installation of a ground-controlled intercept radar system at TTR. This picture was taken in November 1987, near the end of his tour of duty. A fireman stands by a Ford P-12 pumper truck, having just hosed down Manclark's MiG-21 at the conclusion of his final flight as squadron commander. (USAF.)

In November 1980, the Red Eagles received their first MiG-23MS for use in Constant Peg. Several MiG-23 aircraft had been tested at Area 51 since 1978, undergoing technical evaluation by the 6513th Test Squadron Red Hats and tactical evaluation by the Red Eagles. Now, they were ready for introduction into the Constant Peg training syllabus alongside the MiG-17 and MiG-21. (USAF.)

The Mach 2–capable MiG-23MS was one of the most-produced and capable Soviet aircraft of the Cold War. It was the first Soviet aircraft to feature variable sweep wings and paved the way for the equally capable MiG-23BN ground-attack variant. Though less maneuverable than the MiG-21, it was faster and, ruggedly built, could be operated from rough airfields. (USAF.)

Two A-10 Warthogs fly formation with a MiG-23MS over Nevada. The Red Eagles pitted their jets against as many different US combat aircraft as possible. Even so, this seems an odd pairing, as the A-10 was specifically designed to destroy heavily armored ground targets such as battle tanks. By 1985, the squadron possessed 10 MiG-23 aircraft, though not all were simultaneously flyable due to maintenance difficulties. (USAF.)

A MiG-23MS banks left in preparation for beginning an extended final approach to the TTR airstrip. The wings are swept forward for low-speed flight. From 1967 to 1985, more than 5,000 MiG-23s were manufactured, used by 28 nations in Eastern Europe, the Middle East, Africa, and Asia. The MiG-23MS was designed for foreign export and was less capable than domestic Soviet versions. (USAF.)

With landing gear down and locked, another MiG-23MS approaches the runway. The insignia on the nose, just ahead of the cockpit, is a Soviet air force symbol denoting excellence in aircraft maintenance. This was both a realistic marking detail and a nod to the Red Eagles maintenance crew that kept these aircraft flying under challenging circumstances. (USAF.)

The Red Eagles managed to acquire several examples of the MiG-23BN ground-attack variant, in which the nose radar was replaced with a laser rangefinder/target-seeker. More than 600 BN models were produced, with most exported to countries in the Middle East, Europe, Asia, and Africa. An improved version was introduced into service as the MiG-27. (USAF.)

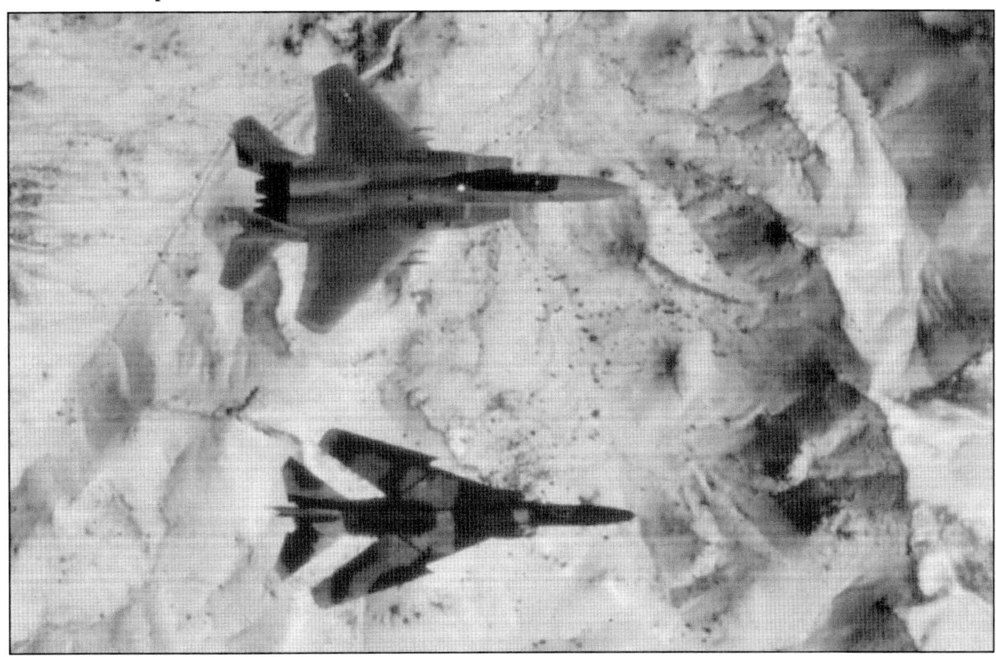

A MiG-23BN, considered by the Red Eagles a challenging and dangerous aircraft, flies formation with an F-15. Capt. Mark Postai died in October 1982 while attempting a deadstick landing in a MiG-23BN following an in-flight fire. In August 1987, Capt. Herbert "Hawk" Carlisle lost control of his MiG-23BN during air combat maneuvers and was forced to eject. (USAF.)

Lt. Col. Robert "Z-Man" Zettel poses next to a MiG-23MS in the spring of 1986. Constant Peg concluded flight operations in March 1988, but the 4477th TES was not completely inactivated until July 1990 and continued, following extensive reorganization, to represent Air Combat Command's interest in USAF foreign materiel exploitation activities. (USAF.)

Squadron personnel pose for a final group photograph shortly before the termination of Constant Peg. Following squadron inactivation, residual assets and personnel were reconstituted as Detachment 2 of the 57th Fighter Wing, continuing the Red Eagles mission on a much smaller scale. In November 1998, the Red Eagles became Detachment 3 of the 53rd Test and Evaluation Group. (USAF.)

Three

NIGHTHAWKS

In 1978, the Air Force awarded Lockheed a full-scale development contract to produce a single-seat, twin-engine jet capable of flying undetected through heavily defended airspace and dropping precision-guided weapons on select targets. Developmental testing took place at Area 51, but TTR was chosen as the permanent base of operations for the new fleet of F-117A stealth fighters under the auspices of the 4450th Tactical Group. (LMSW.)

These officers comprised the first cadre of pilots assigned to the 4450th TG, which began moving personnel to TTR in June 1981. The first operational F-117A was accepted in August 1982, with initial operational capability established 14 months later. The group included a squadron of A-7s at Nellis and two F-117A squadrons at TTR, dubbed the Nightstalkers and the Grim Reapers. (USAF.)

Air Force personnel were ferried to and from the base on chartered 727 aircraft, arriving on Monday mornings and returning to Nellis on Friday evenings, and billeted at the man camp throughout their stay. Secrecy precluded them from telling their families where they were going or what they were doing during the workweek. (USAF.)

Initially, the F-117A was so secret that few top government and military leaders were even aware of its existence. Until it was declassified in 1988, a cover story for the existence of the 4450th TG was provided by a squadron of A-7D attack aircraft being used for "avionics testing" from Nellis. This A-7 two-ship formation is flying over Hoover Dam. (USAF.)

Security for the stealth fighter was serious business. The F-117A was developed and procured within an unacknowledged special access program called Senior Trend. Even within the walls of secure meeting rooms, personnel involved did not typically call the airplane by its official designation, instead obliquely referring to it as "the asset" or "the black jet." (LMSW.)

Stealth pilots attend a pre-mission briefing. From left to right are Maj. Mike Mahar, operations officer; Capt. Skeeter Kohntopp, scheduler; Capt. Terry Foley, flight commander; Capt. Michael Mahan, scheduler; Maj. Rich Treadway, flight commander; Capt. Greg Verser, flight commander; Capt. Steve Troyer, flight commander; and Maj. Mike Daniels, operations officer. (USAF.)

F-117A flight operations initially took place only at night. This was logical, since the aircraft was intended to perform operational missions under cover of darkness, but it also prevented unauthorized observers from spotting the secret jet. One of the airplane's unique characteristics was its faceted shape, designed to minimize its radar signature. (LMSW.)

A pilot steps to his F-117A, officially named the Nighthawk, for an early-evening departure. An operational nighttime flight schedule necessitated that aircrew slept during the day and flew training missions at all hours of the night. On weekends, they returned to their families, reversing their sleep cycle for a few days before returning to TTR to start all over again. This took a physical and psychological toll, with some stealth pilots complaining that they could not shake feeling tired. At first, sorties were restricted to within the boundaries of the Nevada Test and Training Range, but requirements for more realistic training scenarios meant flying beyond the range boundaries and performing simulated real-world missions. This began with mock bombing runs over Las Vegas to target selected buildings in an urban setting. Eventually, the 4450th started flying missions against unfamiliar targets farther from TTR in Utah, Idaho, and California. (LMSW.)

Intense nighttime flight operations were a leading factor in two fatal mishaps during routine training sorties. In July 1986, Maj. Ross Mulhare flew his F-117A into the side of a mountain near Bakersfield, California. Some 15 months later, Maj. Mike Stewart crashed in the desert east of TTR. In both cases, the primary cause appeared to be a combination of fatigue and spatial disorientation. (LMSW.)

For security reasons, Nighthawks were required to be inside their individual hangars by dawn following training missions to avoid being seen by unauthorized observers on the ground or spy satellites overhead. Each hangar was open on both ends for rapid ingress and egress to minimize exposure time. (LMSW via Terry Panopalis.)

Assistant Secretary of Defense Dan Howard publicly unveiled the F-117A at a Pentagon press conference on November 10, 1988. This announcement cleared the way for daylight flight operations at TTR. Night missions were still part of the syllabus, but the new schedule reduced the chances of excessive pilot fatigue. (LMSW.)

In October 1989, the 4450th TG was inactivated and its personnel and assets transferred to the 37th Tactical Fighter Wing, which had just relocated to TTR. Administratively, the wing was divided into the 415th Tactical Fighter Squadron, 416th Tactical Fighter Squadron, and 417th Tactical Fighter Training Squadron (TFTS). The Nighthawk made its combat debut over Panama in December 1989 during Operation Just Cause. (LMSW.)

While the south end of the TTR flight line included hangars and ramp space for the Red Eagles, the 4450th TG housed its fleet in 54 individual hangars specially constructed for its use on the north end of the airfield. Personnel access to the highly secure compound required a palm print scan for entry. (LMSW.)

Parallel rows of F-117A hangars were called "canyons." There were three such canyons, designated from north to south as Red, White, and Blue, each one assigned to a different squadron. Pictured here is White Canyon, consisting of hangars 43 through 54. This group housed the 417th TFTS. (LMSW via Terry Panopalis.)

To reduce the Nighthawk's radar signature, the faceted shape of the F-117A was designed to reflect incident radar waves away from the adversary's receiver antenna, and the periphery of the airframe consisted of radar-absorbent structures. Additionally, the airplane's skin was covered with radar-absorbent material that converted microwave energy into heat that quickly dissipated. (LMSW.)

The wings and tail fins were also faceted, quite unlike conventional airfoils. Radar-absorbent screens covered the engine air inlets to prevent reflections from the jet's compressor face. Flattened exhaust ducts cooled outflowing air to reduce the infrared signature. Four nose probes provided airspeed and altitude data to the flight computer. (USAF.)

The 37th TFW replaced aging A-7Ds with AT-38B trainers for safety chase and for proficiency flights. Note the heavy security at the flight line perimeter. Two fences topped with barbed wire were separated by a well-lit, intensely monitored no-man's land. Armed security guards observed ingress and egress, and the concrete taxiway at the outer gate was marked with a red "Do Not Cross" line. (USAF.)

The F-117A fleet was supported by nine logistics and field service depots under the name Pacer Sprite, designated PS-11 through PS-99. The field service group was known as the Blue Streak Team. PS-66 was activated at TTR on July 16, 1982, and the first field service representatives arrived in October concurrently with the first operational F-117A. (LMSW.)

Col. Al Whitley led the 37th TFW on its first major combat deployment, to the Persian Gulf. During Operation Desert Storm, two squadrons of Nighthawks flew 1,300 combat sorties over Iraq. Over the span of 43 days, F-117A pilots dropped 2,000 tons of precision-guided munitions, scoring 1,600 direct hits in more than 400 locations without losing a single aircraft to hostile fire. (USAF.)

The 37th TFW was inactivated at TTR in July 1992. Remaining personnel and aircraft were transferred to the 49th Fighter Wing at Holloman Air Force Base. At the same time, the 554th Support Squadron was activated at TTR to administer the drawdown of the airfield to custodial status. The DoD approved use of the facility by military and contractor test forces on a temporary, noncontinuous basis. (USAF.)

Nighthawks return to their roost on April 22, 2008. Although most retired Air Force planes go to the Aerospace Maintenance and Regeneration Center near Tucson, Arizona, some still-classified aspects of the F-117A necessitated a more secure location. In December 2006, pilots from the 49th Wing began ferrying the aircraft back to their original secure facilities at TTR. The last two arrived in August 2008. (USAF.)

Most of the retired Nighthawks at TTR had their wings removed for storage in batches of five inside hangars once used by the 417th TFTS. Per Congressional direction within the fiscal year 2007 National Defense Authorization Act, the aircraft were placed in Type 1000 flyable storage for potential recall to future service. (USAF.)

Although some F-117A airframes were scrapped and others put on display in museums, a few Nighthawks were spotted flying over TTR and elsewhere throughout the ensuing decade following their official retirement. At least one of these wore the name of the Dark Knights, a highly classified squadron that might have been using the F-117A in the same way the 4450th TG used the A-7D. (Author's collection.)

In September 2005, the 57th Operations Group activated the 30th Reconnaissance Squadron (RS) at TTR to integrate advanced remotely piloted aircraft systems into the nation's war-fighting capabilities. Among these, the squadron tested and fielded the Lockheed Martin RQ-170 Sentinel, which was developed to provide reconnaissance and surveillance support to forward-deployed combat forces. In August 2011, the 30th RS moved to Creech Air Force Base, Nevada. (Marco Dirkx.)

The vast area encompassed by TTR requires workers to make long commutes from home to the base if they live in Tonopah. Even those living in the dormitories have a long way to go to reach their workstations. Government-operated buses transport military and contractor personnel to remote locations around the range.

An F-16 banks sharply over a Soviet-made MAZ-543P-TEL Scud missile launcher during Exercise Roving Sands. Several of these launchers and accompanying support vehicles were deployed at locations around TTR to simulate enemy threats for US and allied aircrews participating in the joint forces exercise in June 2000. The Scud system is a common threat in the Middle East and Southwest Asia. (USAF.)

Sandia explosives designer Manny Vigil, left, and project lead John Andersen pose with the largest known conical shaped charge (CSC) ever built. Air Force specifications called for punching a hole through at least 15 feet of hard rock. Such projects typically take several years for conceptual design, modeling, analysis, fabrication, developmental testing, peer review, and documentation. Andersen's team accomplished all of these tasks in less than five months.

The Sandia CSC was intended for use with a bunker-buster weapon that was needed so quickly there was only time for one test, which was conducted on November 23, 2002. The charge created a constant-diameter hole 10 inches wide and at least 19 feet deep through a layer of volcanic tuff. The object at upper right is a 96-inch-long instrumented BLU-109 penetrator that was suspended above the CSC.

The TTR airfield remained under the control of Air Combat Command but provided hangar space and support to test organizations assigned to Air Force Materiel Command under Detachment 3, AFFTC. Following the departure of the 30th RS to Creech Air Force Base, ACC transferred responsibility for the base to AFMC and Detachment 3 in 2012. (Gabe Zeifman.)

An anonymous white Boeing 737, unmarked except for a red stripe along the fuselage, taxies past the control tower. Using the radio call sign "Janet," these wide-body passenger transports provide regular commuter service among Las Vegas, TTR, Area 51, Palmdale, and other locations that support classified aerospace projects. (Trevor Paglen.)

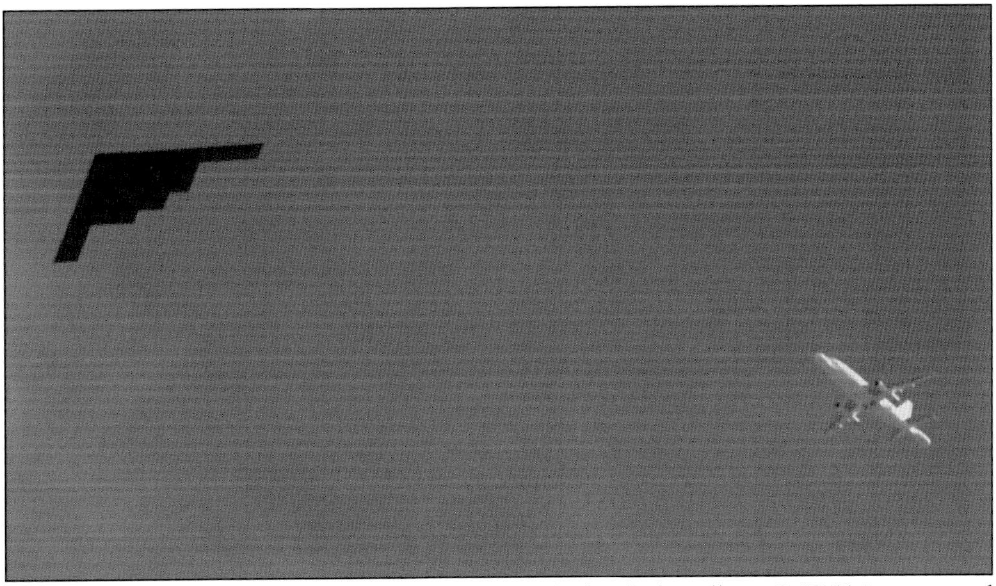

The Air Force operates a modified T-43A as a radar testbed with the call sign RAT-55. It is equipped with radar imaging gear on its nose and tail in radomes that are nine feet long and more than six feet in diameter. RAT-55 is used to make diagnostic radar images of stealthy aircraft such as the B-2, seen here in January 2003. (Brian Lockett.)

Data from the highly-modified RAT-55 are used to evaluate a target aircraft's stealth characteristics in order to determine the rate of degradation of radar-absorbing materials as the aircraft ages and to determine the effectiveness of maintenance and repair methods. (USAF.)

Site 4 at TTR was built as a component of the Tonopah Electronic Combat Range (TECR), which features electronic threats that include surface-to-air missile sites with numerous anti-aircraft artillery fire-control radars that emit an array of signals in as realistic a configuration as possible to simulate an adversary's integrated air defense system. (Gabe Zeifman.)

The vast expanse of the TECR contains a wide variety of electronic threat systems, some sourced from cash-strapped former Soviet republics and others manufactured domestically to simulate foreign equipment. These systems support a flexible, realistic, and multidimensional battlespace for testing new electronic warfare tactics and conducting advanced combat training. (Gabe Zeifman.)

Relics of a bygone era dot the TTR landscape. Within just a few miles of the most advanced modern aerospace vehicles and radar systems lie numerous abandoned mines, deserted houses, and derelict equipment from a previous century. There are several ghost towns in the region, including the Urania Mine, Mellan, and Silverbow. The name of the latter became the radio call sign for TTR.

With all of the technology at TTR, it is sometimes difficult to remember that the range is also part of Nevada's vast open landscape. It is home to a wide variety of wildlife, including pronghorn antelope, gray fox, coyote, and mule deer, as well as a sizable wild horse and burro population that is closely monitored by the Bureau of Land Management.